UNDERSTANDING
WILLIAM H. GASS

Understanding Contemporary American Literature
Matthew J. Bruccoli, Series Editor

Volumes on

Edward Albee • Nicholson Baker • John Barth • Donald Barthelme
The Beats • The Black Mountain Poets • Robert Bly
Raymond Carver • Fred Chappell • Chicano Literature
Contemporary American Drama
Contemporary American Horror Fiction
Contemporary American Literary Theory
Contemporary American Science Fiction
Contemporary Chicana Literature
James Dickey • E. L. Doctorow • John Gardner • George Garrett
John Hawkes • Joseph Heller • Lillian Hellman • John Irving
Randall Jarrell • William Kennedy • Jack Kerouac
Ursula K. Le Guin • Denise Levertov • Bernard Malamud
Bobbie Ann Mason • Jill McCorkle • Carson McCullers
W. S. Merwin • Arthur Miller • Toni Morrison's Fiction
Vladimir Nabokov • Gloria Naylor • Joyce Carol Oates
Tim O'Brien • Flannery O'Connor • Cynthia Ozick
Walker Percy • Katherine Anne Porter • Reynolds Price
Annie Proulx • Thomas Pynchon • Theodore Roethke
Philip Roth • May Sarton • Hubert Selby, Jr. • Mary Lee Settle
Neil Simon • Isaac Bashevis Singer • Jane Smiley
Gary Snyder • William Stafford • Anne Tyler
Kurt Vonnegut • Robert Penn Warren • James Welch
Eudora Welty • Tennessee Williams • August Wilson

UNDERSTANDING
WILLIAM H. GASS

H. L. Hix

University of South Carolina Press

© 2002 University of South Carolina

Published in Columbia, South Carolina, by the
University of South Carolina Press

Manufactured in the United States of America

06 05 04 03 02   5 4 3 2 1

Library of Congress Cataloging-in-Publication Data

Hix, H. L.
　Understanding William H. Gass / H. L. Hix.
　　p. cm. — (Understanding contemporary American literature)
　Includes bibliographical references and index.
　ISBN 1-57003-472-9 (cloth : alk. paper)
　1. Gass, William H., 1924–　—Criticism and interpretation.
　2. Experimental fiction, American—History and criticism.
　I. Title. II. Series.
　PS3557.A845 Z67 2002
　813'.54—dc21　　　　　　　　　　　　　　　　2002001051

CONTENTS

Editor's Preface vii

Preface ix

List of Abbreviations xi

    Chapter 1 Understanding William H. Gass 1

    Chapter 2 Four Characters in *Omensetter's Luck* 6

    Chapter 3 Five Stories: *In the Heart of the Heart of the Country* 30

    Chapter 4 One Theme in Three Essays 51

    Chapter 5 Two Shades of Blue: *Willie Masters' Lonesome Wife* and *On Being Blue* 62

    Chapter 6 Twenty Questions on *The Tunnel* 76

    Chapter 7 Four Movements: *Cartesian Sonata* 140

Notes 157

Bibliography 173

Index 183

EDITOR'S PREFACE

The volumes of *Understanding Contemporary American Literature* have been planned as guides or companions for students as well as good nonacademic readers. The editor and publisher perceive a need for these volumes because much of the influential contemporary literature makes special demands. Uninitiated readers encounter difficulty in approaching works that depart from the traditional forms and techniques of prose and poetry. Literature relies on conventions, but the conventions keep evolving; new writers form their own conventions—which in time may become familiar. Put simply, *UCAL* provides instruction in how to read certain contemporary writers—identifying and explicating their material, themes, use of language, point of view, structures, symbolism, and responses to experience.

The word *understanding* in the titles was deliberately chosen. Many willing readers lack an adequate understanding of how contemporary literature works; that is, what the author is attempting to express and the means by which it is conveyed. Although the criticism and analysis in the series have been aimed at a level of general accessibility, these introductory volumes are meant to be applied in conjunction with the works they cover. They do not provide a substitute for the works and authors they introduce, but rather prepare the reader for more profitable literary experiences.

M. J. B.

PREFACE

Echoing E. M. Cioran's view that "we must read not to understand others but to understand ourselves," William H. Gass warns in an interview that "most critics tend to suppose that they interpret the book, but I prefer to think that the book interprets them and that they should be ready to be interpreted." In writing this book, I have taken that warning seriously, as a standard for my work and for his. If I fulfill the admonition implicit in his words, then the project of understanding William H. Gass should prove a project also of self-understanding.

I am indebted to several individuals and institutions for their help with this book. Lorin Cuoco, Associate Director of the International Writers Center at Washington University, facilitated my research there. Access to Yale University's Sterling Library greatly simplified the remaining research, and the National Endowment for the Humanities made that access possible through its Summer Seminar program. As with each book I have written, my wife, Sheila Pedigo, has been muse and partner, my not without whom.

ABBREVIATIONS

- *CS*   *Cartesian Sonata* (1998)
- *FAF*   *Finding a Form* (1996)
- *FFL*   *Fiction and the Figures of Life* (1970)
- *HHC*   *In the Heart of the Heart of the Country* (1968)
- *HW*   *Habitations of the Word* (1984)
- *RR*   *Reading Rilke* (1999)
- *WWW*   *The World within the Word* (1978)

UNDERSTANDING
WILLIAM H. GASS

CHAPTER ONE

Understanding William H. Gass

William H. Gass claims that he writes "to get even."[1] But with whom, and for what? Nothing in his adult life as a writer and professor appears plausible as a motivation for revenge: his circumstances have been, to all appearances, comfortable, even privileged; he has been given many honors; and his work has been read widely and received well. More likely, then, Gass writes to get even for his childhood, his resentment for which he has clearly stated, as when he calls childhood "a civil war" with "no victors, no peace table, no medals, no quarter," a war that "must be fought to a draw or everyone loses" (*HW,* 130). Everyone in *his* childhood, he implies, did lose—especially himself.

In a statement that links his learning of literary ideals with his coming to understand his own anger, Gass confirms one effect of that loss: "I trust hate more than love," he says, since hate "is frequently constructive, despite the propaganda to the contrary; it is less frequently practiced by hypocrites; it is more clearly understood; it is painfully purchased and therefore often earned; and its objects almost always deserve their fate."[2] Consequently, his writings, especially his fiction, read as if they had been calculated to confirm Czeslaw Milosz's speculation that "there is no other memory than the memory of wounds,"[3] or to dramatize the continuing power of what Elias Canetti calls "the sting," the submerged wound, caused by subjection to others, that never diminishes, remaining "stored up for ever," and that "no child, not even the most ordinary, forgets or forgives."[4]

Gass was born in Fargo, North Dakota, on July 30, 1924. His father, William Bernard Gass, served in the U.S. Balloon Corps during World

War I, taught mechanical drawing at Warren (Ohio) High School, and for extra money played minor league baseball in the Northern League in the summers.[5] He later suffered from debilitating arthritis, but Gass's description makes his father sound more mentally than physically crippled: "He was a right-wing, bigoted person," someone "who read magazines and newspapers in order to find someone to hate. He'd say terrible things about blacks and Jews and 'bohunks.' The depth of his bitterness scared me."[6] Gass describes his mother, Claire (née Sorensen) Gass, as an alcoholic with an extraordinarily passive personality, "a puddle of silence."

Gass describes his childhood as miserable and damaging: "For a long time I was simply emotionally unable to handle my parents' illnesses," he confesses, "I just fled." The consequence for his writing was a rejection of his childhood. "All along one principal motivation behind my writing has been to be other than the person I am. To cancel the consequences of the past."[7] His desire to get even for his childhood shows itself clearly in his fiction, where the two features he identifies as the defining characteristics of his parents, bigotry (father) and alcoholism (mother), recur repeatedly. Besides Gass's explicit description of his mother in his essay "The Doomed in Their Sinking," the first and longest story in *In the Heart of the Heart of the Country,* "The Pedersen Kid," features an alcoholic father; *Omensetter's Luck* stars the hard-hearted Furber; Kohler, the narrator of *The Tunnel,* spews out 652 pages of bitterness and bigotry; and Luther Penner, subject of "The Master of Secret Revenges," the last novella in *Cartesian Sonata,* could hardly be more quick to hate. Gass never forgave or forgot, and the recurrence of characters who so importantly resemble each other and Gass's parents puts the lie to his protestation that "I have nothing I want to tell anybody."[8]

UNDERSTANDING WILLIAM H. GASS

Even before his childhood was over, Gass had decided to become a writer. According to his self-descriptions, his writing skills developed late, but his determination to write emerged early. "I was not precocious in any sense, and it would be hard to say exactly what year I wanted to be a writer, but 8 or 9 or whatever. . . . Certainly by the time I was in junior high school it was absolutely settled in my mind to be a writer."[9]

Gass considers himself primarily a fiction writer, even though he believes that writing fiction "is harder and people are less interested in it, they much prefer my essays." Fiction, he says, is still "far more important to me"; it is "what I really want to write."[10] His university education, though, was in philosophy, not literature or creative writing. He attended Kenyon College and Ohio Wesleyan University, then served in the Navy for three years (a time he describes as the most unhappy period in his life),[11] and returned to Kenyon, from which he received his A.B. in philosophy in 1947. At the time, Kenyon was known across the country as a "headquarters" of the New Criticism. And although Gass only audited courses with one of the New Criticism's main proponents, John Crowe Ransom, he still counts New Criticism among his primary influences.[12] He also identifies as an early influence the positivist tradition in philosophy (also dominant in American universities at the time Gass was a student), with its "great emphasis on logic, the philosophy of science, linguistic analysis, and the idea of very close reading." Gass says of New Criticism and positivism that "the two together certainly determined my attitudes."[13]

Gass earned his Ph.D. in philosophy from Cornell in 1954, writing a dissertation on metaphor under the supervision of Max Black. His time at Cornell coincided with the presence there of two formidable figures in Gass's fields, the novelist Vladimir Nabokov and the philosopher Ludwig Wittgenstein. Though he did not study with either, they were important enough to have cast a shadow over all who came after them, and certainly they count among Gass's most crucial formative influences.

In 1952, Gass married his first wife, Mary Pat O'Kelly, with whom he had two sons and a daughter before ultimately divorcing. During the time he was pursuing his Ph.D., he taught at the College of Wooster in Ohio. In 1955, he was hired as assistant professor of philosophy at Purdue University, where he taught until 1969, when (despite his claim that "I am not a philosopher at all")[14] he was hired as professor of philosophy at Washington University in St. Louis. In that same year, he married his current wife, Mary Alice Henderson, with whom he had twin daughters. In 1979, Washington University appointed him the David May Distinguished University Professor in the Humanities and, in 1990, the director of the International Writers Center. Gass retired from teaching in 1999, but he remains a professor emeritus at Washington University.

Gass has written prolifically, publishing nearly one hundred essays and reviews beyond those collected in his several books of criticism. Still he claims that writing is not easy for him,[15] and certainly his major works have taken long periods to gestate. *Omensetter's Luck* was begun in 1951, but was not published until 1966; the first story in *In the Heart of the Heart of the Country* was written in 1951, though the collection did not appear until 1968; and Gass began writing *The Tunnel* by 1966,[16] but the novel was not published in its entirety until 1995. Gass reports having been preoccupied with Rilke nearly his whole adult life, indeed seldom letting a day pass without reading some Rilke, this although he did not publish his book *Reading Rilke* until 1999.

Gass's numerous awards include the Longview Foundation Prize for Fiction (1959); grants from the Rockefeller Foundation (1965) and the Guggenheim Foundation (1970); teaching awards from Purdue and from Washington University, and the Chicago Tribune Award in 1978 as one of the ten best teachers in the Big Ten; honorary doctorates from Kenyon College, George Washington University, and Purdue University; election to the American Academy and Institute of Arts and Letters (1983); the National Book Critics Circle Award for Criticism in 1985 for *Habitations of the Word* and again in 1997 for *Finding a Form;* the American Book Award for *The Tunnel* (1996); the Lannan Lifetime Achievement Award (1997); and the PEN/Nabokov Award (2000).

CHAPTER TWO

Four Characters in *Omensetter's Luck*

William H. Gass reports that his characters emerge from their names, and his stories from their titles. "I never conceive a character and then seek to christen it. I always have to have the words," he says. "I can't even get a story going until I have the title."[1] His first novel almost certainly originated in just that way, since "Brackett Omensetter" is so distinctive a name, and *Omensetter's Luck* sounds so similar to the titles of older allegories like *Pilgrim's Progress,* where the moral view encapsulated in the character's name and the title dictate the direction of the story.

Even within the novel, the narrator asks, "Didn't a man grow like his name in the long run, and wasn't there a piece of him wedged in it," and "What if Romeo's name were Bob?" (132). Or again, "Suppose God's name was Simpson" (133). Omensetter's name may support this treatment of names as revelatory, but the book's title, *Omensetter's Luck,* misleads the reader in at least one way, by suggesting that Omensetter will be the featured character; in fact "it is the Reverend Jethro Furber, for all his perversion and duplicity, who takes center stage in *Omensetter's Luck,*" rather than "the prelapsarian, preconscious Brackett Omensetter," who remains only "a hollow, a seductive, impossible dream."[2]

Omensetter does have power, enough initially to draw and hold the attention of the other characters, but in Gass's fiction having power matters less than having words. "In my books," Gass says, "if anybody gets to be the hero, he's got the best passages," and because Furber ended up with the best lines in *Omensetter's Luck,* he "is what

FOUR CHARACTERS IN *OMENSETTER'S LUCK*

the book turned out eventually to be all about." Omensetter, in contrast, "is certainly not the major figure, because he is basically a person without language. He is a wall everybody bounces a ball off."[3] Omensetter is not *un*important, since the other characters, "the devoted chronicler, the worshipper, the opponent," do group themselves around him, and they "must see an extraordinary power in him, otherwise they would not stop to chronicle, worship, or oppose."[4] It is just that, instead of being the main character, Omensetter occasions the thoughts and words and actions of the main character. It is as if the book were named not by Gass but by Furber, and not after the character who preoccupies the writer—that would be Furber—but after the character who preoccupies all the other characters.

In this way, *Omensetter's Luck* exemplifies "metafiction" (fiction *about* fiction), a category into which Gass's work is often placed. The writer creates fictional characters who themselves create a fictional character, Omensetter, who is "more fictional" than they are. Their creation of this character not only occurs within the fiction of the novel, but acts as a commentary on the nature of fiction in general. Because "Omensetter is an ideal created through the perceptions and words" of Tott, Pimber, and Furber, who therefore "have written Omensetter's wonders themselves," those characters, Tott, Pimber, and Furber, act in a way that mimics reality. "In attempting to give form to Omensetter, Gass's characters give form instead to themselves—they 'essay to be.' What they become is not transcendental 'transparent eyeballs,' but fuller, more realistic human beings who recognize the limitations of consciousness."[5] All of Gass's characters attempt to become the authors of a life, and Tott, Pimber, and Furber achieve that aim; their failure is that, though they author someone else's life, they fail to successfully author their own.

Letting the characters, rather than the writer, choose the title, and letting the writer's characters produce another character of their own, would be appropriate to the book's content, since character rather than plot drives *Omensetter's Luck,* giving the novel its order and momentum. The characters Israbestis Tott, Henry Pimber, and Jethro Furber, in keeping with Gass's emphasis on words, assume responsibility "for the generation of the novel's language. Each of their perceptions dominates a section of the novel, with the largest by far belonging to Furber, the most polished and professional monologist among them."[6] The narrative moves, as Aristotle's *Poetics* says complex plots always do, toward a discovery, "a change from ignorance to knowledge,"[7] but *Omensetter's Luck* doubles the discovery: Omensetter discovers that his luck is not reliable when his contact with Furber initiates him into conscious reflection, and the reader discovers the order and meaning of the events not because an omniscient narrator reveals their order and meaning, or because they produce a reversal as sudden and overwhelming as in Aristotle's favorite example, *Oedipus Rex,* but through the reader's own mental compilation of the biased, fragmentary views of the three narrators. Each narrator is unreliable, but together their testimonies can be weighed one against the other to infer a more reliable understanding.

1. Israbestis Tott

The first section attends to Israbestis Tott, a character who exemplifies the weight Gass gives to names. His name might be taken to mean something like, "the addle-headed person who struggles with animals." The Hebrew name "Israel," given to Jacob after his wrestling with the angel in Genesis 32, and now used eponymously to name the Hebrew people and their home country, means "he who strives

FOUR CHARACTERS IN *OMENSETTER'S LUCK*

with God," and "Isra" is the part that means "he who strives." The second half of Tott's first name appears to come from the Latin "bestia," the root of English words like "beast" and "bestial." And "Tott," though it may derive, as Larry McCaffery suggests, from the German word "Tod," which means "death,"[8] certainly echoes the obsolete English word "tot," which the *Oxford English Dictionary* defines as "a person of disordered brain, a simpleton, a fool," and the still widely-used word "totter" (a word that appears in Tott's section, on the very first page of the book), with their implications of instability.

Tott's introductory section "acts in much the same way that an overture does for a musical composition; here all of the novel's major characters and events are introduced briefly and obliquely, along with most of its important symbolic and thematic patterns."[9] Or in Gass's own words, "Tott as a story comes first so that we'll know how to evaluate the rest."[10] Set many years after the events that occupy the rest of the book have occurred, Tott's section names Omensetter and confirms through reference to the river's regular flooding and the cradle of Omensetter's child what the book's title already suggests, namely that Omensetter's luck functions as the axis around which the events revolve. Tott's section identifies Pimber and refers to the lockjaw of which Omensetter cured him; it also introduces the Reverend Jethro Furber, suggesting from the first mention his role as the serpent in the garden by having Israbestis recall that, at their first handshake when Furber arrived in town, "the Reverend's arm reached out and bit him" (13).

Tott fancies himself "the town historian," and he "tries to chronicle [Omensetter's] impact on the town."[11] At the auction of "Missus Pimber's things," Tott keeps trying to find someone who will listen to his recollections, repeatedly claiming that he "saw this house go up," and telling, or trying to tell, anyone who will listen the story of when Bob

Stout, who built the Pimbers' house, "fell from the Methodist steeple" onto the iron fence (10–11). But though the stories are all the ground Tott has to stand on, they cannot support him. He can reassure himself that "There was the story of the man who went to pieces, and there was the story of the high and iron fence. There was the saga of Uncle Simon, the Hen Woods burning, and the hunt for Hog Bellman. He had them all." He can brag that "Hours, weeks, months—a life—they'd cost him." But then he must ask immediately, "Were they all as wrong as the one about the cradle?" (22–23). Without yet knowing the story about the cradle, the reader does learn from Tott that the story ends badly, and that Omensetter's luck runs out with his son's illness.

Tott's stories in fact *are* all as wrong as his version of the story about the cradle. Arthur M. Saltzman calls Tott "a spider tangled in his fictions," adding that, although Tott's story does not end in a literal human death, it does end "with Tott crushing a 'nasty' spider with his thumb, symbolically uniting his limited and limiting brand of art with death."[12] Tott commits a kind of artistic (and therefore both intellectual and moral) suicide by meeting neither of two opposed standards. He does not represent the world accurately and "realistically," nor does he create an autonomous and successful artifice. A reader would be gullible to believe his stories or be drawn to his character. "To the degree we have a positive feeling for Tott, to that degree we have been sucked in—are like him," says Gass. "Tott loves Omensetter as a figure in a story. Lots love Jesus for no other reason."[13] Like so many of the characters in Gass's various fictions, Tott tries to make a world of words, but does not succeed.

In contrast to Tott himself, the narrator of the Tott section *does* succeed, with vivid and lilting sentences like those describing the crowd at the auction of Lucy Pimber's estate: "On the shaded porch the women squeezed themselves between card tables set with tilting towers of china cups, bubbled colored glass and painted plates. In the back, by the barn, the men gathered in serious pairs to smoke, heft heavy implements, and think" (10). However, the narrator's success in creating a world of words consists, in part at least, of showing Tott's failure to do so. Tott tells "tale after tale," telling each one "many times over, getting them right or trying to, amazed at what he forgot and what he remembered. There was a secret in every one and he tried to discover it" (18). Tried, but did not succeed. Tott gets interrupted often, as when he first tells the iron fence story, and barely manages to get out, "It was funny about the fence because—" before he is interrupted (11). Sometimes he loses his audience, as when the kid he talks to longer than anyone else says suddenly, "I got to go. That's my ma," and after a few more interchanges prompted by Tott's attempts to coax him into staying, finally just says, "Bye" (28). Sometimes Tott simply fails to maintain his own concentration, as when the crowd overwhelms him (22). Tott fails by the aesthetic criterion suggested by the boy he talks to, that "good stories are long," and also by his own related criterion that "I always put everything in" the story. Tott never manages a long story, or a story with everything in it; he accomplishes the narrator's ends by failing at his own.

2. Henry Pimber

Unlike Tott, Henry Pimber "is *too* successful at creating his own verbal image of Omensetter."[14] His image is an ideal, so far from reality that Pimber allows it to disorient him and to corrupt his self-understanding. Pimber meets Omensetter through Mat the blacksmith, who tells Omensetter that Pimber has "a house which might be rented since it was empty and dissolving and sat like a frog on the edge of the river" (34). That the house floods regularly does not deter Omensetter, who has arrived, after all, in an uncovered wagon, despite the recent rains. Omensetter seems allied with water from Pimber's first sight of him: his "dark hair fell across his face and he'd tracked mud on the porch, but his voice was musical and sweet as water, his moist lips smiled around his words, his eyes glimmered" (34).[15] When Pimber cautions that they don't normally rent the house at this (rainy, flood-prone) time of year and that the house is "near to the river," Omensetter dismisses the warning by saying of his family that "we all love the water" (35). Pimber falls under Omensetter's spell immediately. Even before they finish their first interchange, Omensetter has "overpowered him, set his fears at rest, met his doubts, and replaced his customary suspiciousness with an almost heedless trust" (34).

The first test of Omensetter's blithe disregard for rain and the river comes quickly, and his luck shows itself. The flood comes "within thirty yards of Omensetter's side yard fence," but even though "more rain had fallen than had in years," this house that has flooded often before does not flood with Omensetter in it. Omensetter's apparent immunity from the dangers of life makes Pimber acutely aware of his own subjection to these dangers. In religious terms, this awareness makes Pimber "the Everyman of the novel. His plight and his desire result from an awareness of the Fall which the seemingly unaffected Omensetter aggravates."[16] In psychological terms, "Pimber sees in Omensetter the lost potential of his own meager life," making Pimber "Omensetter's psychic opposite."[17] Omensetter's immunity from danger grants him a freedom from worry and from the need for foresight that makes him seem to Pimber "foolish, dirty, [and] careless,"

FOUR CHARACTERS IN *OMENSETTER'S LUCK*

and liberates him from subjection to social customs. Omensetter "ate lunch with his eyes shut; and, needless to say, he laughed a lot. He let his hair grow; he only intermittently shaved; who knew if he washed; and when he went to pee, he simply let his pants drop" (38).

The incident that reveals most dramatically the contrast between Pimber and Omensetter occurs when Pimber comes in person ("because his wife insisted") to collect the rent, and discovers Omensetter's daughters dancing, as if in a pagan rite, around the well, into which a fox has fallen while trying to escape with a stolen hen. "The hen lay dead by the open well and the dog crouched growling at its lip," and Omensetter shows Henry how "the eyes of the fox reflect the moon" (38). Henry asks how Omensetter plans to get the fox out of the well, but Omensetter says, "He'll have to stay where he's put." Henry recognizes it as Omensetter's luck "for the fox to seize the bitterest hen, gag on her as he fled, and then fall stupidly to the ground" (39). But Omensetter's refusal to liberate the fox puts Pimber in a panic. Pimber's "reasoning here is as follows:

> I am in this well like the fox is.
> Only Omensetter can save me.
> <u>Omensetter won't save the fox.</u>
> Omensetter won't save me either."[18]

Pimber's immediate fascination with the fox overwhelms him. He sympathizes with the fox, worrying that "the fox must be badly bruised, terribly cramped, his nose pressed into the damp well wall" (39). He sees the fox, wholly within nature, as akin to Omensetter, and therefore as an accuser who points to Pimber's own fallenness: "The fox *out* of the well is identified with Omensetter. The fox *in* the well with Henry."[19] When Omensetter looks in the well, he sees the moon reflected; when Henry looks, the strength of his identification with the fox is such that he sees himself reflected. "Animals felt pain, he understood, but never sorrow." Pimber lives "fearfully; but such a creature as the fox filled up the edges of its body like a lake. . . . You could startle an animal, but never surprise" (40). The fox reminds Pimber of the contrast between his own worrisome struggles and Omensetter's unmitigated ease: "What Omensetter did," Pimber muses, "he did so simply that it seemed a miracle. It eased from him, his life did, like the smooth broad crayon line of the man who drew your cartoon at the fair" (42), unlike Pimber's own life, which emerges only accompanied by intense labor pains, and with a hyperactive conscience that leads to persistent second-guessing.

The strength of Pimber's reaction to the fox, though, follows from his identification with its situation, in which he sees "the horror of his own imprisonment."[20] Pimber cannot help but ask, "Suppose he'd fallen there himself?" (41), but the supposition causes a "horrified reaction" that "results from his sympathetic identification with what is happening to the fox, whose life is now as enclosed and threatened as Pimber's own existence. Henry's imaginative recreation of how the fox feels trapped in the well" becomes a "projection of his own imprisonment; Henry senses the similarity of their 'falls' as he rushes home to get a gun with which he can put the fox out of its misery"[21] by shooting it "with both barrels" (43).

Pimber seeks relief, but shooting the fox grants him none. Killing the fox gives Pimber "the same fierce heedless kind of joy" accompanied by illness and guilt that he recalled from a childhood incident in which he struck his father "a terrible blow in the stomach," but this time he knows that "it was Omensetter he had struck at" (43), not the fox. As

FOUR CHARACTERS IN *OMENSETTER'S LUCK*

in other fictions by Gass ("The Pedersen Kid," *The Tunnel*), so in *Omensetter's Luck,* the conflict between father and son figures prominently.

In thus striking at giants, men who are literally (his father) and figuratively (Omensetter) larger than himself, Pimber makes himself a figure of the biblical David. This comparison becomes explicit when, after killing the fox, Henry sits beside the river "passing five white carefully gathered stones from hand to hand" (43). In the book of Samuel (1 Samuel 17), the biblical David persuades Saul to let him challenge Goliath by describing how he has killed lions and bears when they have threatened his flock, and he readies himself for the fight by gathering "five smooth stones." David's stones, though, because of his courage and divine favor, bring him victory, but when Pimber throws his stones they kill no giants and bring no victory: "One sank in the water's edge; one clicked on a greater stone; one found the sand; another bruised the marsh weeds. The last lay at his feet like a dead moth" (44). Pimber ends the fox's life with a bang, but the reader realizes Pimber's own life will end with a whimper.

Stones become important to Pimber, who longs (as he longs to be a fox, or Omensetter, or indeed anything other than himself) to be a stone, "to be hard and cold again and have no feeling" (57). Repeatedly, stones remind Pimber of his own state, as when, following Omensetter into the woods, Henry "sat on a rock and pulled his coat around him," but without relief, because "the cold stone pressed against him" (59). Or when in self-condemnation he imagines himself "dead of weak will and dishonest weather," but without a stone to mark his grave, concluding that "I shall be my own stone, then, . . . my own dumb memorial" (60).

Pimber becomes like the stones: cold, motionless, and lifeless. In contrast, Omensetter makes the stones like himself: animate and free. "Omensetter's stones," when he skipped them on the river, "dipped and flew and lit like gulls upon the water" (65). These two characteristics, Pimber's tendency to become like stones, and Omensetter's ability to animate stones, contest each other in the incident of Pimber's lockjaw: the disease makes Pimber stonelike, and Omensetter, by curing Pimber, animates him. Though unintentional, the wound that brings on the tetanus is self-inflicted, a result of shooting the fox: one of the shot pellets ricochets off the stones in the well and grazes Pimber's arm. "At first the wound was merely sore and then the arm was stiff," and then the stiffness—the stoniness—"spread into the neck" (44). Omensetter draws on his connection to nature, making "a poultice of mashed raw red beet" and binding it to the wound. Eventually Dr. Orcutt arrives and removes the poultice, administering more orthodox medication ("opium and aconite," and "lobelia and capsicum" [45]). Furber stays to pray for the patient. Pimber recovers ("the jaw was loose by morning"), even though Dr. Orcutt confesses that he would have "sworn it was hopeless," and everyone attributes the healing to Omensetter; but the cure from lockjaw only delays, and does not prevent, Pimber's becoming stonelike.

Although Pimber's eventual end is revealed in Furber's section rather than in Pimber's own, it still relates to the incident of the fox. Pimber "chooses to reverse the death of the fox, his spiritual double, by hanging dead from a tall tree limb instead of down a dark hole."[22] Just as Pimber's recovery from lockjaw consolidated the community around Omensetter, to whom they attributed the cure, Pimber's hanging consolidates the community against Omensetter, because (accustomed now to attributing all extraordinary events to his power) they suspect him of having caused it. In this way, as in many others, Omensetter's luck reveals its double edge. Unusual ability of any sort may offer possibilities, but it also imposes a burden and poses a threat. "People whose gift will not break / live by it all their lives; it shadows / every empty act they undertake."[23] Omensetter's blessings come from his luck, but so do his curses.

3. Jethro Furber

Pimber's section is longer than Tott's, but by far the largest portion of *Omensetter's Luck* is devoted to "The Reverend Jethro Furber's Change of Heart." Furber, the town's preacher, a strict and pious man, wears a religious exterior that covers a turbulent inner life. Gass says in "A Letter to the Editor" that Furber "has been sent to Gilean by his church for unspecified but guessable misdemeanors. He is bitter and revengeful to begin with" (101). Like Pimber, Furber is simultaneously drawn to and repelled by Omensetter, but if Pimber's attraction/repulsion grows out of wonder, Furber's grows out of rancor.

Furber, "Omensetter's opposite, a man whose profession involves him completely in a world of words and abstractions,"[24] resents Omensetter's irreligious, natural, joyful freedom, the way "every Sunday Omensetter strolled by the river with his wife, his daughters, and his dog. They came by wagon, spoke to people who were off to church, and while Furber preached, they sprawled in the gravel and trailed their feet in the water" (67). Omensetter possesses, and (as Furber sees things) threatens to infect Furber's congregation with, a pre-verbal joy that prompts inarticulate and unselfconscious grunts and guffaws from the people as they play: "Heya-heya-heya. Someone climbing. Rocks pitched after a board; and on the river, tilting patches of reflection. Heya-fulla-heya-heya." Or again, "Hiyah-smilah. Hee-mee? Coltch. Skirts rose slowly, slowly subsided. A parasol flew open with a snap. Or-rawk. Gah. Houf. Half-buried in the shingle, a deep red brick was then awash. Yo-yo giggy. Teetoo. Sheek? Num! Lissa-lissa" (69). Omensetter possesses and transmits the childlikeness praised in the gospels.

In contrast, Furber finds himself all too adult, always articulate and overly self-conscious, able to do nothing but speak. Furber, whose character shows clearly in the incident in which he acts out with shadows a fantasy of making love with a woman on a train ("the shadow of his hand descended on the lap of the thick young lady sitting next to him" and his fingers "burrowed toward her privacy" [108]), embodies Blake's assertion that "he who desires but acts not, breeds pestilence,"[25] and indicates "how imprisoned Furber is within his own powers of perception and language."[26] Omensetter cannot rival Furber's capacity for speech, but he does not need to because his happiness is complete without speech. Unhappiness, according to Rousseau, derives from "the disproportion between our desires and our faculties," but a person "whose faculties equaled his desires would be an absolutely happy being."[27]

What others call luck in Omensetter, Rousseau would describe as a match between Omensetter's faculties and his desires. In the terms of Furber's religion, the same match could be named grace, a concept that Gass claims implicitly inhabits the book under an assumed name. "A metaphor need not be stated to be present. In *Omensetter's Luck,* the idea of grace (never directly discussed) is ironically represented by the idea of luck."[28] Furber's frustration, his incapacity to receive grace, derives from the fact that his desires so far outstrip his faculties. The stretch of stream-of-consciousness prose that follows Furber's observation of the people playing by the river reveals that his frustration "would nearly always end like this—

FOUR CHARACTERS IN *OMENSETTER'S LUCK*

with an outburst of speech" (71), but the outbursts are themselves frustrating rather than satisfying. His capacity for speech cannot bridge the chasm between his desires and his faculties.

Furber exemplifies what Gass calls "the verbal sexualization of the mind," a state in which "the language becomes so eroticized" that the character begins "making love with words," until "everything that comes into him falls into a nest of images that transform it in that way."[29] Even in front of his congregation everything falls into that nest, as when, speaking on the biblical creation story in Genesis, he drifts into using a metaphor of seduction/rape by God. "Just as God in the beginning had divided the darkness to make light, stealing on it while it lay asleep, and just as God had taken the sweetness from the sea as it rested to vault the sky," he preaches to them, "so mankind was also divided in slumber, and the darkness taken, and a portion of the divine breath too, to make a wife" (173). Furber makes love with words in both of the senses of that sentence: he makes love by using words in place of his body, and he makes love to words. Words are for him both the instruments and the objects of his affection.

Furber does not merely fail to practice what he preaches; he doesn't practice at all. In Furber, the problem is that he preaches one thing aloud (to others) and another silently (to himself). Furber's flaw receives one explanation in Gass's essay "On Talking to Oneself," where Gass argues that "to think for yourself—not narrowly, but rather as a mind—you must be able to talk to yourself: well, openly, and at length" (*HW,* 213). The internal dialogue, "this secret, obsessive, often silly, nearly continuous voice," is the very "center of the self," and "the surest sign that we are alive" (*HW,* 215). Like Hamlet, Furber maintains an ongoing inner dialogue. However, Hamlet manages to talk to himself "well, openly, and at length." He "escapes his circumstances and achieves greatness despite the fact his will wavers," not "because he has an Oedipus complex" but "because he talks to himself more beautifully than anyone else almost ever has" (*HW,* 212). Furber only manages to talk to himself at length, but not openly or well.

Gass himself calls Furber's speeches "Hamletish," and says they suggest a syllogism: "God is omnipotent and omnipresent; He made and is in all things. What, of all these things, shows him to us best? He cannot display his power best in making good, because he is good. Only by making evil. God is evident most in the Devil. And the Devil, being a master of deceit, hides himself in the Good. So what appears good is evil, and what is evil is most like God." The syllogism is "dialectical nonsense," but that does not prevent its governing "the movement of the images throughout,"[30] or keep it from continuing to disclose Furber's nature. "Like a waterstrider, Furber rode a thin film of sense" (174).

That "thin film of sense" might also be characterized, using a more common metaphor, as a "web of deception," since Furber has no scruples that incline him to honesty. He "knows all too well that lying is his only skill,"[31] but lying creates verbal artefacts and has existential consequences no less than does truth-telling, and his possession of heightened verbal skills (as reflected in his trade, which centers on sermons, as well as the internal monologue to which readers have access) makes Furber's lying particularly effective. In fact, lying rather than truth-telling produces what Carolyn J. Allen calls Furber's "greatest achievement," his "creation of the myth of Omensetter," a task in which "Furber succeeds in a way he never suspects," a way that exceeds any expectations he could have harbored: "Omensetter himself believes it."[32]

FOUR CHARACTERS IN *OMENSETTER'S LUCK*

That disparity between what Furber expected and what he caused, the surprising realization that his lies proved true, creates his unique situation in the novel. "Furber is confronted," Gass says, "by the fact that his own system of ideas might really be true. I mean, it was okay to believe it as long as it really *wasn't so*. That's true for a lot of people. Beliefs are held in a very strange way." Furber undergoes a change of heart because "his rhetoric is brought home. It was tolerable as long as it was held in rhetorical abeyance, but as soon as it becomes more than that, it becomes intolerable."[33]

Since speech has defined Furber from the beginning, his "change of heart" is marked by a change in his manner of speech, a very specific alteration in the way he pronounces Omensetter's first name. From the start of Furber's section, his "continual mispronunciation of Omensetter's name (he refers to him as 'Backett') is one of the key indications that he is *not* in touch with Omensetter's true nature,"[34] but at the moment of his transformation he pronounces Brackett's name correctly for the first time. Omensetter has confided to Furber—with his usual naiveté and unsuspecting trust—his discovery of Pimber's corpse in the tree. Furber does not believe Omensetter, but Omensetter says, "All that matters is you trust me," to which Furber cannot help but say, "What a godforsaken soul I have. Ba—Brackett—what a shit I am" (191). For at least a brief moment, Furber speaks the truth to himself and to someone else.

In this way, Furber resembles Claudius, the usurping king from *Hamlet*. Both ill-willed souls play roles of substitute fatherhood, and both come to regret their wickedness. Claudius confesses his sins in act 3 scene 3, in the soliloquy/prayer that begins, "O, my offense is rank, it smells to heaven." Even though Claudius wants forgiveness, he knows he cannot have it, "since I am still possessed / Of those effects" for which he committed his crimes, and he recognizes himself as a "limèd soul, that struggling to be free / Art more engaged." In Furber's case, it is the narrator who confesses that Furber "had fathered every folly, every sin. No goat knew gluttony like his, no cat had felt his pride, no crow his avarice" (206). Like Claudius, who tries to pray, Furber makes gestures in the direction of redemption by saying "the psalm against envy, the psalm against anger," but like Claudius, who cannot overcome his guilt, for Furber the psalms "were no defense." Finally, like Claudius, who becomes identified with "offense's gilded hand," Furber had "labored on the Devil's side as if the Lord Himself had begged it of him."[35]

In *Hamlet,* Hamlet is more articulate than Claudius, so Claudius fears that Hamlet will win the support of others, depriving Claudius of his external power base and, ultimately, of his life; in *Omensetter's Luck,* Furber is more articulate than Omensetter, so Furber fears the loss of his command of language. He fears, in other words, that Omensetter's nature will infect his own, a fear whose realization Furber the preacher puts in religious terms: "I am inhabited, Furber said. Ah god, I am possessed" (116).

Trying to exorcise the spirit/demon of Omensetter, Furber initiates a confrontation by seeking out "Omensetter himself when Omensetter was strolling in the fields" (an ironic echo of the biblical creation story when Adam and Eve, having eaten the forbidden fruit and become aware of their nakedness, "heard the sound of the Lord God walking in the garden," and "hid themselves from the presence of the Lord God" [Gen. 3:8–9]). Furber tries to cast out Omensetter. "Why do you inhabit me, he cried, why do you possess my tongue and turn it from the way it wants to go? Leave me, Omensetter, leave us all" (116).

FOUR CHARACTERS IN *OMENSETTER'S LUCK*

The confrontation does not have the effect Furber has desired; Omensetter "had not come to church again," returning instead "to skipping stones on the river" (117). As it was in Pimber's section, so in Furber's: Omensetter's ability to animate stones receives repeated emphasis. "It was truly astonishing," the narrator says, "the way his stones would leap free of the water and disappear into the glare. Omensetter always chose them carefully. He took their weight in his palm and recorded their edges with his fingers, juggling a number as he walked and tossing the failures down before he curled his index finger around their rims and released them as birds" (117). Stones realize most fully in Furber's section the role of representing Omensetter's life-giving capacity that they practice in Pimber's section. "Through the medium of Furber's thoughts," Margaret Dornfeld points out, the stones serve "a crucial symbolic function. Each stone, originally the epitome of lifelessness, seemed to draw vitality from Omensetter's touch. Omensetter's ability to animate these stones reflects his role in the novel as a life source," so the stones represent the same "power to bestow life" that manifests itself "in the cure of Henry Pimber."[36]

On the one hand, the fixedness of stones is a vehicle for one tenor of the metaphor. In Watson L. Holloway's words, "The idea of stone as symbolic of the numinous, transcendent self, a lasting permanence in the face of death's obliteration, appears extensively in *Omensetter's Luck;* it is the principal image in the novel."[37] The characters themselves are depicted as if they were aware of this on some level. After he has been accused of murdering Pimber, and after his boy has become sick, Omensetter tries to arrange the stones in a circle, a Stonehenge in diminuendo, moving "on all fours like some nocturnal animal," merely "gathering stones" instead of vigorously flinging them as he had previously. "On a patch of cleared ground above the beach Omensetter set the stones in piles to form a circle," and then "stood in the middle, swaying, as dark and vague as any of the trees" (207). His action "mimics Furber's reliance on sanctuary,"[38] which prompts Furber to run "about the circle kicking at the piles." Omensetter's arranging the stones and Furber's destroying the arrangement indicate shared recognition of the stones' symbolizing solidity and "permanence in the face of death's obliteration."

On the other hand, as Holloway points out only a few pages later, the capacity of stones for movement, given the right force, is also significant: "The throwing of stones is a ritual repeated throughout the novel. Omensetter seems to give life and weightlessness to the dead weight of rocks as he makes them skip across the water" (37). Holloway calls Omensetter's rock throwing a "ritual" and observes its opposition to Furber's religious practices, noting that it "provides a natural, primitive, pagan counterweight to Furber's word throwing inside the church" (37). Like the book as a whole, Furber attempts "to apprehend natural order through verbal order," but the natural order refuses to be apprehended in those terms, no matter how many words Furber throws.[39] Stones reveal that Omensetter embodies in his inarticulate and irreligious life precisely what Furber purports—falsely—to offer through his articulate and religious speech. Whether "skipping stones across the water, or sending horseshoes into the air, Omensetter entices Furber with the possibility of transcendence of human mortality."[40]

4. The Ohio

James McCourt has suggested reading Gass's later novel *The Tunnel* as a retelling of Shakespeare's *Hamlet*,[41] but important parallels with

FOUR CHARACTERS IN *OMENSETTER'S LUCK*

Hamlet already appear, long before *The Tunnel,* in *Omensetter's Luck.* In addition to the echoes pointed out earlier in this chapter, Tott, Pimber, and Furber each must face Omensetter's luck, just as Hamlet, Laertes, and Fortinbras each must face a father's murder. Just as in *Hamlet,* each character is defined by his reaction to the problem, and its contrast with the reactions of the other characters.[42]

A fourth character, however, has gone largely unnoticed by critics, although the effect of the book depends on its role. Like Tott, Pimber, and Furber, this fourth character, the Ohio River, receives definition in part by its relation to Omensetter's Luck. A river is not a human being, obviously, but in his essay "The Concept of Character in Fiction" Gass makes a point of saying that, though characters *may* be human, they need not be. They only *have* to be fixed points in narratives, "primary substances to which everything else is attached" (*FFL,* 49), so even though "normally, characters are fictional human beings," there are other possibilities. "A symbol like the cross can be a character. An idea or a situation. . . , or a particular event, an obsessive thought, a decision. . . , a passion, a memory, the weather, Gogol's overcoat—anything, indeed, which serves as a fixed point, like a stone in a stream or that soap in Bloom's pocket, functions as a character" (*FFL,* 50). It would be hard to miss the irony in the Ohio's fulfilling a function defined by fixedness, since the river's salient characteristic is perpetual movement and flux; but, flowing or not, the river occupies a place in Gass's narrative as fixed as that of any human character.

The Ohio acts in Gass's novel very like fate in a Greek tragedy: without appearing on stage, it looms behind all the events and helps determine their meaning. In this regard *Omensetter's Luck* exemplifies a characteristic Northrop Frye attributes to tragedy. Even though "the tragic hero is very great as compared to us," as Omensetter at least appears to the other characters to be, "there is something else, something on the side of him opposite the audience, compared to which he is small. This something else may be called God, gods, fate, accident," and so on.[43] Its names vary, Frye says, "but the form in which it manifests itself is fairly constant." It enforces on tragedy, as it enforces on *Omensetter's Luck,* "an epiphany of law, of that which is and must be" (208). The righting of natural balance, what the Greeks called *nemesis,* occurs "impersonally, unaffected, as *Oedipus Tyrannus* illustrates, by the moral quality of human motivation involved" (209). In *Omensetter's Luck,* the river embodies that impetus toward the restoration of natural balance, enforcing on the human characters the indifferent necessity of nature.

Gass has emphasized in interviews that he did *not* make the Ohio River the setting of the novel for historical or geographical reasons. He did not want to make the work "realistic," rather he wanted to "create a work that can be read nonreferentially." Instead of aiming for realism, "I wanted to take on the nature-culture cliché because I knew that it was one of the basic themes of American literature, and I wanted to have my go at it. I set *Omensetter* back in that particular period precisely because I *didn't* want my writing to be influenced by reality." Gass consciously tried to avoid realism, and believes he succeeded. "If anybody looked at the book carefully, I think they would see that it really says nothing at all about the 1890s, nothing about the Ohio river towns, of which I have no knowledge whatsoever."[44] Gass wants the same names, "Ohio" and "the Ohio," that we normally use to designate a real geographical region and a real river, respectively, to refer in the story to nothing real, nothing outside the story. "*Omensetter* isn't really set in Ohio" at all, Gass says, and "that is the point."[45] The river, then, does not serve

FOUR CHARACTERS IN *OMENSETTER'S LUCK*

primarily to give the book the illusion of reality by allowing the details of a familiar setting to orient and comfort the reader; Gass argues often in his essays against the worth of that illusion. On the contrary, Gass uses the river to make the book more mythical by emphasizing the setting's metaphorical role.

The significance of the Ohio River to *Omensetter's Luck* receives its clearest statement not in the secondary literature or explicitly in the novel itself or in the author's commentary on the novel, but in an essay that initially might seem unrelated, Gass's essay on a different river, the Mississippi. That essay begins, "To live by a river is to live by an image of Time,"[46] adding the related observations that "a river is nothing but unintended destination," and, "when we compare Time to a river, it is because we wish both were moving elsewhere than fatally to a Gulf" (1). Gass goes on in that essay to note other salient features of major rivers like the Mississippi and the Ohio. For one thing, they "lend themselves to the cyclical view of history, surging and waning with the seasons, but above all passing their waters along to the oceans where the sun's rays raise the moisture up" until its "skyborne waters fall as rain till rivulets run into rivers again" (3). The river has definite effects on humans: "everything the water touched was loosened in its moral fiber; waterfronts grew riffraff as naturally as frogs and rib grass" until "not even the bluffs were far enough away for the good folk, who withdrew from the region altogether" (10–11).

The river, Gass says, "is primeval energy itself." No matter what we do, "the river goes. When we walled and banked and dredged and tanked it, . . . the river went right on," just as the Asian proverb says it will: "Nations die / rivers go on / mountains / go on."[47] Now, despite our pleasure boats and vacation cottages and water skiers, "the river turns its wide brown shoulder, shrugs off such shenanigans, and continues what it's always done," knowing that "its business is to wax and wane as much and as often as the moon does" (16).

The river, then, represents the presence of the inevitable. The characters are most obviously aware of the river as the source of inevitable chaos, as when it rises within a few feet of Omensetter's house, and more generally by the annual threat of destructive flooding. Chaos is not the only inevitable state, though, and—like providence itself—the river can be the source of peace, as it is in Tott's memory of the days when "they would sit in the boat and fish in the river. The trees hung over and shaded the sides. They would drift in and out of the shade, eddying with the river, watching the cork float, their broad hats tilted, shading their eyes." When they drifted out of the current, "Lloyd would reach up and pull on a limb and the boat would coast out into the sun again where the water sparkled and slapped gently against the hull. It was warm and comfortable and there weren't many fish, but just slow and easy drifting down by the checkered river" (14). The river's peace extends beyond summer through all the seasons: "In winter one could see quite easily through the gate at the end of the garden to the river lying placidly in its ice—leaden, grave, immortal" (64).

In addition to asserting the presence of the inevitable, whether as chaos or peace, the river, echoing the river that "flows out of Eden to water the garden" in the biblical creation narrative, sets up the Eden myth that permeates the novel, which becomes "a working out of the basic metaphor of art and culture: the myth of Adam and Eve and the Garden."[48] The town of Gilean, continuing Gass's emphasis on the significance of names, helps to evoke the Eden myth by mimicking the biblical locations of Gibeon and Gilead. Even as Henry Pimber denies the correspondence between Omensetter and Adam, the narrator, taking advantage of the unreliability of Henry's point of view,

FOUR CHARACTERS IN *OMENSETTER'S LUCK*

establishes the correspondence. Henry wonders, "Had he thought they were playing at Adam and Eve? three children and a dog? PARADISE BY RIVERSIDE" (58), and concludes "Not Adam but inhuman."

The Eden myth transforms the whole novel into a narrative of a fall (or of *the* fall), and if it makes it possible for Furber's concluding biblical role to be as a repentant Judas returning the "thirty pieces of silver" to Mrs. Pimber, it makes inevitable that the Omensetters— Adam and Eve—had to be driven from the garden, moving "down river—children, horse, dog, wife, and wagon—no one knew quite where" (236).

CHAPTER THREE

Five Stories: *In the Heart of the Heart of the Country*

In his *Poetics,* Aristotle names six components of a narrative, identifying plot as the most important of the six. To make the point, he contrasts plot with character (another of the six ingredients) as a way of showing why the former matters more. Aristotle argues that "character gives us qualities, but it is in our actions—what we do—that we are happy or the reverse." Stories do not portray action in order to display their characters, but instead employ characters in order to make action possible. Plot, Aristotle argues, is the end, character merely the means. A story "is impossible without action, but there may be one without character."[1]

William Gass adopts the opposing point of view, contending that "great character is the most obvious single mark of great literature" (*FFL,* 35), and reversing Aristotle's hierarchy to make plot the means and character the end: "The purpose of a literary work is the capture of consciousness," the replication, in other words, of what a character thinks and feels, rather than how he or she acts, "and the consequent creation, in you, of an imagined sensibility, so that while you read you are" not the observer of events but "that patient pool or cataract of concepts which the author has constructed" (*FFL,* 33). Gass also specifically identifies the privileging of character over plot as an evaluative criterion to be applied to his own work, suggesting that "if I alter any reader's consciousness, it will be because I have constructed a consciousness of which others may wish to become aware, or even, for a short time, share" (*FAF,* 47), not because he has portrayed actions others may wish to observe or even participate in.

FIVE STORIES: *IN THE HEART OF THE HEART OF THE COUNTRY*

The previous chapter portrayed character as central to *Omensetter's Luck*. Character also holds pride of place in all five stories in *In the Heart of the Heart of the Country* and creates the point of greatest continuity between the two books. In fact, the degree of similarity between the characters in each leads Watson L. Holloway to call the narrators of the stories in *In the Heart of the Heart of the Country* the "offspring or subspecies of Jethro Furber," citing as family resemblances that "they are alienated; they peer at their surroundings through screens made of language; they hide behind windows and doors and look out at things."[2] The continuity from character to character also extends beyond these books; besides echoing those in *Omensetter's Luck,* the characters in these stories also anticipate the characters in each of Gass's later fictions, including Babs in *Willie Masters' Lonesome Wife,* Kohler in *The Tunnel,* and characters like Riff and Emma in *Cartesian Sonata.*

Gass confesses an autobiographical origin to the retreat into language that so many of his characters share. He himself was taught, he says, "to deflect my desires from their real object onto another, safer, simpler one" and "to alter myself rather than the world," for which tasks he discovered that he "had one facility: I had, on my side, a little language." Using that facility, he says, "I read to escape my condition, I wrote to remedy it," with the result that "there is scarcely a significant character in my work who is not a failure in the practice of ordinary existence, who does not lead a deflected life. Often, though not always, they live inside a language, and try to protect themselves from every danger with a phrase" (*FAF,* 32–33).

That the characters share a feature with their author, though, matters less than that they share it among themselves, and the main characters in *In the Heart of the Heart of the Country* "burrow into themselves and make up aesthetic and ontological systems from their obsessive word flows." Because each narrator finds solace in language (rather than, for instance, assertive action, as one would expect if Gass agreed with Aristotle about the preeminence of plot), each becomes "a mind in retreat, or, as the unnamed storyteller in the concluding story refers to himself, an eye driven inward" in an attempt "to secure a reliable refuge" that can serve "as an alternative to a world characterized as violent, tedious, loveless, or downright inscrutable."[3]

The recurrence of this character type gives the stories a shared set of concerns, and means that "the usual subject of the tales is, in one word, immanence; it is their usual object to make ordinary things and events become luminous with the evidence of a supreme and metaphysical order."[4] Or, to put the matter in another way, in these stories the world shrinks down to the size of the visual field of the speaker, as in one of Gass's philosophical mentors, Wittgenstein, where the assertion that "the limits of my language mean the limits of my world" is followed almost immediately by the correlative that "the subject," Wittgenstein's equivalent to one of Gass's narrators, "is a limit of the world."[5] Ordinary things in these stories may grow as big as the world; and, conversely, the world shrinks to the size of the most ordinary thing. The world contracts into the cold moldy basement in "The Pedersen Kid," a few adjacent houses in "Mrs. Mean," Fender's cramped living room in "Icicles," the downstairs of the narrator's house in "Order of Insects," and "a small town fastened to a field" in the title story.

1. The Pedersen Kid

Tony Tanner treats "The Pedersen Kid" as an exception, saying of only the four *other* stories that they "are centred upon lonely observers

FIVE STORIES: *IN THE HEART OF THE HEART OF THE COUNTRY*

('wondrous watchmen'), obsessed, prurient, passively curious, isolates of the eye, and mind, and word."[6] Tanner is only half right. "The Pedersen Kid" *is* an exception to the subordination of plot, but certainly not an exception when it comes to character: the protagonist, Jorge Segren, despite his youth, matches perfectly the traits Tanner attributes to characters in the other stories but withholds from him.

Jorge displays, for example, a Freudian obsessiveness, as is suggested even in the first few sentences, where the reader sees Hans "carrying something from the crib" (1). Choosing the *crib,* with that word's evocation of nativity, instead of the *trough,* say, or a *stall,* transforms the story's opening into a thinly "disguised birth scene," by the end of which "Jorge's role has been usurped," causing a "disruption in family dynamics," the result of which, "Freud claims, is always resentment." The reader knows from the onset, then, that the Pedersen kid will pose a psychological threat to Jorge, and that "a timeless battle is being reenacted, a battle as old as Cain and Abel."[7] The first element of Freud's Oedipus complex, rivalry for the mother's affection, begins early in the story, too, when in the second paragraph "Ma" is first depicted caring intently for the Pedersen kid, "fumbling with the kid's clothes" and making "a sound like whew from every breath" (1), while ignoring Jorge, who can only watch and take commands.

The other element of the Oedipus complex, conflict with the father, receives its introduction next, when Jorge has to rouse his father from a drunken sleep in order to get whiskey to help warm the kid, knowing that his father will be angry and violent over being wakened and over the need to disclose one of the hiding places where he keeps a bottle. This conflict becomes amplified over the course of the story. The latter anger is not just over losing the whiskey and the hiding place itself, but over the damage to his ego. "He took pride in his hiding. It was all the pride he had" (8). Pa's sensitivity on the issue of hiding whiskey culminates in a conflict with Big Hans. When, after learning that Ma and Big Hans had already administered some whiskey to the Pedersen kid even before Pa revealed any hiding places, Pa asks where they got the whiskey, Hans replies,

> Oh Hed found it. You don't hide worth a damn and Hed found it easy. She knew right away where to look.
> Shut up, Hans, I said.
> Hans tilted the bottle.
> She must have known where it was a long time now. Maybe she knows where they're all hid. You ain't very smart. Or maybe she's took it up herself, eh? And it ain't yours at all, maybe that.
> Big Hans poured himself a drink. Then Pa kicked the glass out of Hans's hand. (31)

Jorge emphasizes Pa's dependence on drink to make a point of his recognition that Pa cares more about whiskey than about Jorge himself, as is dramatized later when the bottle gets bumped out of Pa's lap into the snow. "Where's my bottle? Pa said, looking over the side of the sleigh at the torn snow. Jorge, go find my bottle. It fell in the snow here somewheres" (36). Jorge's attempt earns no gratitude. "I kicked about. Pa followed my feet" (37). Jorge experiences his father's indifference toward him with a perfect clarity of understanding.

So, even though "Jorge, like his pre-Christian forebear Oedipus, must kill his father" because he "is Magnus, 'mighty one,'" and as such "emblematic of all fathers,"[8] Jorge hates him not only *as* a

FIVE STORIES: *IN THE HEART OF THE HEART OF THE COUNTRY*

representative of all fathers, but also as this particular indifferent, drunken, abusive father. Jorge's hatred finds expression, long before Pa gets shot, in the repeated conjunction between Pa and feces. "Even more frequently than he is associated with horses, Pa is associated with excrement—with shit."[9] The pattern begins early in the story, where the third sentence out of Pa's mouth is "A fat turd to Big Hans" (5), followed soon by "I shittin well understand" and a reminder of an incident in which he dumped his chamberpot, in which he had "been shit-sick," on Big Hans; the pattern recurs throughout the story.

Jorge's prurience, like the other elements of his character, shows up early in the story. Having acted with studied indifference while Ma and Big Hans tried to save the kid's life and prevent frostbite, Jorge first shows interest in the Pedersen kid when he gets the chance to compare penis size. "By now the kid was naked. I was satisfied mine was bigger" (2).

The "passively curious" characteristic, though, occupies center stage, because the story develops like a mystery. As Melanie Eckford-Prossor's penetrating reading reveals, "The Pedersen Kid" investigates "three realms of 'knowledge': fact (whatever that may be—perhaps the 'fact' of the kid's death—and the story shows us precisely the way empirical 'fact' may be denied and how subject it is to interpretation), belief (in the face of fact and in the rightness of one's actions), and imagination (as a way of providing alternatives to 'facts'—Jorge's skating 'in' to his imagination)." Confronted by "the three main questions posed by the text—Who shot Pa? What happened to the Pedersen family? and Is there really a Yellow Hands?," Jorge's curiosity is engaged.[10]

The kid, whose condition would cast doubt on his testimony even if it were not improbable-sounding on its own, gives little information, and Jorge gets the information second-hand, through Hans's mumbling. "That's all he says he saw, Hans said, staring at the mark of the kid's behind in the dough. Just his back. The green mackinaw. The black stocking cap. The yellow gloves. The gun" (14). Jorge asks, "That's all?," and it is, but it proves plenty to mobilize Hans. The *im*probability, though, not the probability, sustains Hans's curiosity; he reasons that the story's combination of clarity and unlikeliness rules out its being a fabrication or a fantasy. "Green, black, yellow: you don't make up them colors neither. You don't make up putting your folks down cellar where they'll freeze. You don't make up his not saying anything the whole time or only seeing his back or exactly what he was wearing. It's more than a make-up; it's more than a dream" (17).

Jorge has to puzzle through Hans's *report* of the kid's story and his *interpretation* of it. Hans talks his way through the kid's story, thinking out loud in front of Ma and Jorge, and concludes that the story must be true. Jorge doubts the story and Hans's basis for accepting it, but his skepticism can't explain away the kid's very real presence. "What Hans said sounded right. It sounded right but it couldn't be right. It just couldn't be. Whatever was right, the Pedersen kid had run off from his pa's place probably late yesterday afternoon when the storm let up, and had turned up at our crib this morning. I knew he was there. I knew that much. I'd held him" (18).

When Pa enters the discussion, he complicates matters by adding a moral imperative from which he exempts himself, but which he says binds Hans if he accepts the kid's story as true. "Seems like it'd be terrible if the Pedersen kid was to have come all that way through the storm, scared and freezing, and you was to have done all that rubbing and saving so he could come to and tell you his fancy tale and have you believe it, if you ain't going to do nothing but sit and hold

FIVE STORIES: *IN THE HEART OF THE HEART OF THE COUNTRY*

hands with that bottle" (23). Having cornered Hans, he goads him with one more consideration in favor of believing the story. "There's a thing to consider, he said, beginning to smile. Why ain't Pedersen here looking for his kid?" (27).

The plot unfolds as the three rival males, Hans, Pa, and Jorge, set out to solve the mystery. In some respects, the story arrives eventually at a clear resolution. The Oedipal drama is fulfilled by the father's death. The rivalry between Jorge and the Pedersen kid finds resolution through a change in Jorge's attitude from competition to emulation.[11] The quest theme is resolved when Jorge enters the Pedersen's house, symbolically occupying the castle. The mystery, though, is never solved. "One can locate several points in the story at which Jorge may have hallucinated the rest,"[12] so none of the last portion of his account can be accepted as reliable. The reader never learns what happens/happened to the Pedersen family, so even though Jorge was driven out of a strictly passive curiosity, the story ends in such a way that the reader's curiosity can never be anything other than passive.

2. Mrs. Mean

In "Mrs. Mean," Gass's narrator reverses the modus operandi of Gass the writer; instead of inventing a character out of her name, he invents a name to match her character. "I call her Mrs. Mean," he says, even though "I don't know her name" (80). The name particularly suits the metafictional impulses of Gass the writer, though, because of its double entendre: "mean" as an adjective means spiteful, base, or common, but as a verb, it means to intend or to signify. The narrator in "Mrs. Mean" makes additional announcements early on of how fictional is the world he describes. "No one has his home here but myself; for I have chosen to be idle, as I said, to surround myself with scenes and pictures; to conjecture, to rest my life upon a web of theory" (81). His neighbors all serve the same purpose for him that blank pages serve for a writer: "I sail my boats on their seas. I rest my stories on their backs"; "I take their souls away—I know it—and I play with them; I puppet them up to something" (83).

All his neighbors serve that purpose except Mrs. Mean, who refuses subjection to his imagination. "However I try, I cannot, like the earth, throw out invisible lines to trap her instincts; turn her north or south; fertilize or not her busy womb; cause her to exhibit the tenderness, even, of ruthless wild things for her wild and ruthless brood. And so she burns and burns before me" (88). Mrs. Mean occupies the narrator's imagination, even *preoccupies* it, but will not submit to it. In that respect, she resembles the very force of nature, with which she is allied. Pejoratively, the narrator represents that alliance through bestiality, calling her "cow-chested, horse-necked, sow-faced" (103). In nobler terms, he presents her "amid constant reference to the four traditional elements of being—heat, moisture, air, and earth—"and therefore as resembling "being itself."[13]

The narrator thinks he is not alone in considering Mrs. Mean intractable. "There have been complaints," he reports, about her chasing her children out of her own yard into those of the neighbors "so she can mow and tamp and water her crop of grass" (90), leaving the children to "tramp the garden down the street" and "run through Mr. Wallace's hedge" (95). The narrator says that "the authorities, more than once, have been notified. Nothing has come of it." He depicts her as maintaining an ongoing monologue of cursing and vituperation aimed at her children: "Damn. Oh damn. You little snot. Wait'll I get hold of you, Tim. You are so little, Tim. You are so snotty, so dirty

FIVE STORIES: *IN THE HEART OF THE HEART OF THE COUNTRY*

snotty, so nasty dirty snotty. Where did you get that? What *is* that? What's it now? Drop that. Don't bring it here. Put it back. Nancy. Witch. Oh jesus, jesus, sweet, sweet jesus. Get. Did you piss in the flowers? Timmy? Timmy, Timmy, Timmy, did you? By god, I'll beat your bottom flat" (91). Unlike the neighbors, though, "the children almost wholly ignore it." Mrs. Mean tends her yard and tries to subdue anything that threatens it, whether dandelions, upon which she "vents her hate" (96), or her own children, whom she treats like dandelions: "although they are quite small children, Mrs. Mean always augments her power with a stick or strap and dedicates to their capture and chastisement the same energy and stubborn singleness of purpose she has given to the destruction of weeds" (98).

In thus failing to distinguish between her own children and common weeds, and tending with more forbearance and attention to her yard than to her children, Mrs. Mean assumes her place in Gass's oeuvre as an early embodiment of one of his recurrent themes: "Evil that is everyday is lost in life, goes shrewdly into it; becomes a part of habitual blood" (101). The habituation and contagion of evil in this story makes the narrator seem almost to be foretelling *The Tunnel*'s mean main character, Kohler, when he opines that "the eldest Mean child may someday say, confronted by a meanness that's his own, by his own mean soul, that he was beaten as a boy; and he may take a certain solace from the fact; he may shift at least a portion of his blame to the ages" (102). The connection between the meanness portrayed in "Mrs. Mean" and that in *The Tunnel* receives further support when the narrator writes that "thorough evil is as bright as perfect good and seems as fair. . . . Real wickedness is rare. Certainly it does not rest in the tawdry murder of millions, even Jews" (113). The relation between the Holocaust and "real wickedness," barely adumbrated in

"Mrs. Mean," becomes the focal meditation in *The Tunnel*. In the meantime, the narrator of "Mrs. Mean" is not shy about expressing his opinion on the matter. "I should like to see Providence take the side of the dandelion. A tooth for a tooth would suit me fine" (108).

The movement of the story, though, pursues another aim. The narrator takes a walk along the alley that feeds the garages behind the houses, and to avoid being noticed by another neighbor he ducks into the Means' garage, then hides beside a tire to avoid being seen by one of the Mean children. Shame at being so compromised leads him to the realization that "I have breached the fortress, yet in doing so I have lost all feeling for the Means and sensed only myself, fearful, hiding from a child" (117). That self-absorption leads him (as if he were passive, being guided by some force other than his own will) into the yard of Mrs. Cramm, one of his neighbors, and he quietly watches her.

The shame and passivity overwhelm him, though, and he realizes that "I am not myself. This is not the world. I have gone too far. It is the way fairy tales begin—with a sudden slip over the rim of reality" into the world of Hänsel and Gretel, who "went for a walk in a real forest but they walked too far" and the real forest became "a forest of story" with a gingerbread house as fictional as the Means' house, and a witch as fantastic as Mrs. Mean (117).

Even though the narrator claims not to have recovered from his trespassing, he concludes the story by confessing his hunger to trespass again. "The desire is as strong as any I have ever had: to see, to feel, to know, and to possess! Shut in my room as I so often am now . . . I try to analyze my feelings," and after the analysis "I know the time is only days before I shall squeeze through the back screen of the Means' house and be inside" (119). The plural reference to all the

FIVE STORIES: *IN THE HEART OF THE HEART OF THE COUNTRY*

Means, collectively, returns the reader's attention to Mrs. Mean's name, by adding a third meaning to the two already noted. Far from manifesting Emersonian self-reliance, the narrator admits here his inability to understand the world and assert his will. He plans to use (and seems to believe he *can* use) his neighbors, especially the Means, as a *means* to the ends of happiness and satisfaction that he knows he will not achieve cloistered in his room with the door shut.

The narrator does not see about himself what the reader can see clearly: that even if he does leave his room and enter the Means' house, he will still be *hiding,* still trying to live surreptitiously, to substitute a pretended life for a real one.

3. Icicles

"Icicles" depicts another character who tries to put something else in place of his life. Bruce Bassoff contrasts "Icicles" with "The Pedersen Kid," observing that "while 'The Pedersen Kid' enacts a sacrifice, an expense that solarizes the world and restores our sense of intimacy, 'Icicles' enacts the contrary process of reification, in which the boundaries between men and things break down." Bassoff concludes by describing "Icicles" as a "parable of reification," in which "people become things."[14]

The process of reification in the story begins with the opinionated Pearson, who "was fond of saying" to the main character, Fender, that "nothing happens—anywhere—that doesn't happen on a piece of property" (125–26). From that purported fact, Pearson's opinions progress to an analogy: "properties were like people, they had characters; they suffered from vicissitudes, as he'd told Fender often, and fell upon evil times like the best of us did, only to rise up again and be renewed as it also happened sometimes." His mastery of the analogy means "that Pearson could, when he drove a street, pass judgment on it, read its future" (127). Pearson's eyes are piercing: whenever and whatever he sees, he knows.

Pearson does not remain content, though, with the analogy between property and humans. Instead, he expands the concept of property until it becomes all-inclusive: "Everything is property. Pearson's face would glow, his hair shake. Everything is property. Think of it" (130). Property includes everything, and it outlasts everything. "People pass on. In the midst of life, you know, Fender . . . well . . . but property, property endures" (130). The objects of Pearson's devotion will never desert him.

Continuing this line of reasoning, that property is a more inclusive category than people, and that the category of property outlasts the individuals in the category of people, Pearson arrives at the inference that "people are property" (130). The unsoundness of his reasoning does not prevent his getting carried away with it and arriving at a reversal of the usual view of the relation between property and people. Pearson holds that "*property owns people*. Everything's property, and the property that lasts longest—it owns what lasts least" (131). Pearson manages what few of Gass's characters achieve: an understanding of the world that *works* for him, that brings him advantages (represented especially by the interest and favor of Isabella, who Fender fancies but cannot attract), and allows him to thrive.

Fender falls for it. "It made sense, yes. It still made sense. But now it did seem a hard saying . . . hard to bear. His little house possessed him, it was true. He'd been cut to fit its walls. He saw what it permitted. He did not reach beyond the rooms. . . . Pearson was right. The question his buyers should have asked—do I want to belong to this house?—they never asked" (131). Fender's problem comes from

FIVE STORIES: *IN THE HEART OF THE HEART OF THE COUNTRY*

his believing that Pearson is right, but not being, in Nietzschean terms, strong enough to live up to the idea. His "character is not equal to the deed,"[15] and that inequality renders him, now in Aristotelian terms, incontinent: he understands the world in one way, but lives in a different way. Unlike Pearson, Fender has not found his own way of understanding the world and living in it.

Fender does *try* to find something to serve as a metaphor the way property serves for Pearson, but Fender's choice, icicles, though they manage to attract his attention, do not possess the stability and durability that property has. "He tried to remember when he'd last paid icicles any mind—in his childhood sometime, surely—but his memory failed him, he was left with a blank. There was a house, doubtless, somewhere, he'd lived in, but he'd lost the address. Even now his life slid swiftly by and was soon out of sight like a stick on a river" (139). If Pearson's objective correlative, property, grounds him and lends stability, Fender's correlatives, icicles, actually unsettle him and remind him through their fugaciousness of his own.

The icicles also leave Fender at the mercy of others, including children. At one point when he is showing some customers a house, "suddenly there were alarming quick steps on the porch. Fender lifted the front shade and a small boy turned toward him and stared in, an icicle every bit as big as he was cradled in his arms. By god, Fender gasped, running toward the door, the nerve!" Leaving his customers, "Fender gave chase, but at once lost his quarry behind the garages" (153). Fender wants to connect his fugitive icicles with Pearson's stable and lasting property, but neither the icicles themselves nor other people will let him do so.

Fender finds his world increasingly "threatened by the world that surrounds him. Caught between these two worlds, Fender can do nothing to save himself."[16] Among other cues that alert the reader to

Fender's despair, Gass identifies him (through the use of allusion) with the narrators in two of T. S. Eliot's major poems, "The Waste Land" and "The Love Song of J. Alfred Prufrock," those paragons of modernist fear and paralysis. "You've no right to weep, Fender, whose fault is it?," the story's last paragraph asks. "His chair held him; he had no energy; he would never sell again; certainly he was sick. What'll you do, then, Fender? What'll you do tomorrow?" (162). The allusion is to "The Waste Land," which asks, "What shall we do tomorrow? / What shall we ever do?"[17] Fender's interior monologue continues: "Tomorrow, he thought. God. The coming hour, the minute following, the second next. Should he sneeze? lift his hand? laugh?" (162), a set of questions that echoes Prufrock's "Shall I part my hair behind? Do I dare to eat a peach?"[18] Literature is often thought of as having progressed from "stock" or "cardboard" characters who are more type than individual (Homer's Hector, for instance) to characters who are more individual than type. Aligning Fender with Eliot's prototypical characters, though, helps Gass reverse the implicit valuation in that view of literary history, and emphasize Fender's being a type over his being an individual.

4. Order of Insects

The pattern of alluding to modernist poetry continues in the next story, whose title invokes as its background one of the most famous lines in modern poetry (from a poem that preoccupied Gass for years), the question Rilke poses at the beginning of his *Duino Elegies:* "Who, if I cried out, would hear me among the orders of angels?"[19] Rilke's poem goes on (in Gass's own translation) to ask, "Isn't it time that we lovingly / freed ourselves from our lovers and, although shaken,

FIVE STORIES: *IN THE HEART OF THE HEART OF THE COUNTRY*

endure it, / as the arrow stands in the string to become, upon its momentous release, / something more than itself?" (*RR,* 190). Both Rilkean questions preoccupy the speaker in the story.

Rilke is not the only major modernist writer echoed by the story, though. When the problem identified in the very first sentence is that "the bodies of a large black bug" are "spotted about the downstairs carpet" (163), Kafka's *Metamorphosis* has been summoned, as Eusebio L. Rodrigues notes when he calls "Order of Insects" a "translation into fiction of Plato's observation that perception is a form of pain. A Kafkalike piece, it focuses on a moment of vision that breaks up a whole way of existence."[20] The old way of existence for the narrator is that of a housewife, and the first thing the bugs do to undercut that existence is to surprise her. "I could not imagine where the bugs had come from. I am terribly meticulous myself. The house was clean, the cupboards tight and orderly, and we never saw one alive" (164). She has been dutifully (and without questioning) performing the tasks she takes as her responsibilities, all centered on keeping the house in order.

The bugs interpose a question about how well she has been keeping order, and more importantly they raise the question of what her motives are or should be for keeping order. The bugs force the question on her: "they are a new experience for me and I think I am grateful for it now" (165). Why grateful? Because she comes to see things differently as a result of the bugs, in a way that sets "Order of Insects" apart from Kafka's *Metamorphosis*. "While Kafka's character must realistically accept the dehumanization of actually becoming a cockroach for the degradation that it is, Gass's housewife, in typical Emersonian fashion, must insist on identification with the bugs as a transcendence and unity with nature."[21] The bugs are not just bugs.

"When I examine my collection now it isn't any longer roaches I observe but gracious order, wholeness, and divinity" (169).

The bugs prompt her to subvert the socially constructed order, according to which she has been living "in a scatter of blocks and children's voices" where "the chores are my clock, and time is every other moment interrupted," in favor of the order of nature that supports self-assertion beyond her social stature, as it supports the bugs' bearing significance beyond their physical stature: "this bug that I hold in my hand and know to be dead is beautiful, and there is a fierce joy in its composition that beggars every other, for its joy is the joy of stone, and it lives in its tomb like a lion" (170).

The analogy between Rilke's order of angels and the story's insects, though, dominates. The speaker in Rilke's poem hears voices, and tells himself to "Listen, Oh, my heart, as hitherto only / holy men have listened. . . . Not that you could bear / the voice of God—far from it. But hear the flowing / melancholy murmur which is shaped out of silence / wafting toward you now from those youthfully dead" (*RR,* 191). The speaker in Gass's story also hears sacred and life-transforming voices, though in this case they come from "the true soul of the roach; a soul so static and intense, so immortally arranged, I felt, while I lay shell-like in our bed, turned inside out, driving my mind away, it was the same as the dark soul of the world itself" (168).

Rilke's angelic voices ask for help maintaining their purity and ethereality. "What do they want of me? that I should gently cleanse them / of the tarnish of despair which hinders a little, / sometimes, the pure passage of their spirits" (*RR,* 191). Gass's narrator hears a similar request from the roaches, whose "bodies dry and the interior flesh decays," but whose "features hold, as I suppose they held in life, an Egyptian determination, for their protective plates are strong and

FIVE STORIES: *IN THE HEART OF THE HEART OF THE COUNTRY*

death must break bones to get in. Now that the heavy soul is gone, the case is light" (166). The empty shells of the insects instruct the narrator about life, until she exclaims, "Alas for us, I want to cry, our bones are secret, showing last, so we must love what perishes: the muscles and the waters and the fats" (166–67). But the insect shells also "suggest metaphorically both death and resurrection."[22]

The narrator recognizes that "this point of view I tremble in is the point of view of a god," but she cannot bring herself to accept the point of view and its existential consequences. She considers herself unworthy of such elevation, and the story ends with her denying the transcendent view in favor of remaining "the wife of the house, concerned for the rug, tidy and punctual, surrounded by blocks" (171).

5. In the Heart of the Heart of the Country

Like "Order of Insects," "In the Heart of the Heart of the Country" alludes from its very beginning to a major modernist poem as its precursor, in this case William Butler Yeats's "Sailing to Byzantium," but this time with a different relationship between poem and story. "Order of Insects" adopts the ideals of the "Duino Elegy" to which it responds, but "In the Heart of the Heart of the Country" contrasts itself to the Yeats poem, standing as the poem's negative. Yeats's Byzantium is sacred, Gass's B profane. "'B' is the diminished, unregenerate version of Byzantium, the eternal city of art."[23]

The allusion itself is more blatant than subtle, but as if to remove any possible doubt Gass affirms its significance with over- rather than understatement. Asked once by an audience member at a public forum, "How far are you carrying that particular reference?" Gass replied: "Well, all the way. It's one of those little private difficulties:

how much the relation to the Yeats poems is involved. Every bloody thing I can lay my hands on," even in the details. "It was pointed out by some anal observer that the sections of the story and the lines of the poem are the same.[24] And that's true. . . . That's a little kind of imposed formality that I did to help shape the work."[25]

The imposed formality serves as an apotropaic to ward off realism. Just as Gass wants *Omensetter's Luck* not to be mistaken for a "realistic" account of a turn-of-the-century Ohio river town, so he wants "In the Heart of the Heart of the Country" to stand as something other than an account of life in a mid-twentieth-century, small midwestern town. "If the story were an account of how it is or was to live in Brookston, Indiana, it would have to be much more extensive and very different. But of course the story isn't about that at all. It's about a mind with very severe limitations, about a psyche whose feelings are full of self-pity, about an eye that's been driven back in."[26] Gass wants the story to be realistic, but not about the *place*. He wants it to be realistic about the *mind* of its speaker, and that speaker's mind, like those of other speakers in Gass's fictions, has a very limited, distorted, deceptive, and otherwise unrealistic apprehension of what he is describing.

The story's points of thematic focus thus are not peculiar to the place, but occur regularly in all the places in which Gass sets his fiction. For example, windows, a recurring metaphor throughout Gass's work, occupy an important role in this story. They trap perceptions, confining what is normally thought of as "free" and "outside." For example, "Leaves move in the windows. I cannot tell you yet how beautiful it is, what it means. But they do move. They move in the glass" (175). The confinement is not only a figurative stasis but a figurative death. "My window," he says, "is a grave, and all that lies

FIVE STORIES: *IN THE HEART OF THE HEART OF THE COUNTRY*

within it's dead" (195). And the confinement includes the perceiver as well as the perceived, so the narrator says he himself only wanders "from room to room, up and down, gazing through most of my forty-one windows" (183). He does not wander out into the world, so the reader gets not a picture of B, but a picture of the narrator's confinement, the view from his cell.

The person given the most attention by the narrator (other than the narrator himself) is Billy Holsclaw, who comes to stand for B in several ways. For one thing, continuing the people/property theme begun in "Icicles," Billy resembles his house, which "shed its paint in its youth, and its boards are a warped and weathered gray" (174). His house is old; Billy is old. His house is dying; Billy is dying. "Billy's like the coal he's found: spilled, mislaid, discarded. The sky's no comfort. His house and his body are dying together. His windows are boarded" (200). Most importantly, though, Billy Holsclaw serves in the story as an Everyman, who stands for *all* the citizens of B. He does what we do, and does it so inevitably that he represents us, even becomes us. "Billy closes his door and carries coal or wood to his fire and closes his eyes, and there's simply no way of knowing how lonely and empty he is or whether he's as vacant and barren and loveless as the rest of us are—here in the heart of the country" (180).

Billy's representativeness means that when the narrator tries to "find a figure in our language which would serve him faithfully, and furnish his poverty and loneliness richly out" (190), he also struggles for *self*-expression. He wants, as do all of Gass's narrators, to find a linguistic figure to furnish out *his own* material and spiritual poverty, as well as his self-imposed loneliness.

The narrator wants to escape the decay he sees around him and feels within him, and this desire manifests itself in various ways. One way is the literary figure, in keeping with the allusion to Yeats. The "wood or plastic iron deer" in the first section is "a mock representative of the artifice of Yeats's Byzantium—a substitute for the natural, sensual world that is subject to decay."[27] Another way is through expressed admiration for the immediacy with which the other inhabitants of that natural, sensual world (the inhabitants other than himself) experience it. His cat, for instance, does not have to *become* a cat. "You are, and are not, a machine. You are alive, alive exactly, and it means nothing to you—much to me. You are a cat—you cannot understand—you are a cat so easily. Your nature is not something you must rise to" (184). Even insects (not surprisingly, given the story that preceded this one) make the narrator jealous. "Flies have always impressed me; they are so persistently alive" (204).

The persistence with which the narrator recognizes that, whatever it does to the rest of the natural world, to him at least "age cannot be kind" (179), completes the story's replication of the Yeats poem to which Gass so closely ties it. The number of sections in the story may match the number of lines in the poem, but the most important correlations run deeper than that. In the words of Frederick Busch's succinct, summary statement, "If we follow the implicit analogy closely, the small town is Byzantium *and* the heart sick with desire; the heart is fastened to a dying animal, the town is fastened to a field. The field, then, the land, the earth, is analogous to a dying animal. Gass's narrator may be trapped in what he has wished to flee: time, which makes the animals—and poets—die."[28] In this way, the narrator of "In the Heart of the Heart of the Country" resembles the other speakers/protagonists in Gass's fiction. Their hearts are fastened to dying animals, but one might twist the Yeatsian language and say, too, that their animals are fastened to dying hearts.

CHAPTER FOUR

One Theme in Three Essays

Near the beginning of the most extensive and acute study to date of Gass's essays, a chapter in her book *Beautiful Theories,* Elizabeth W. Bruss calls William Gass "not an especially original literary theorist," just a tenacious one: Gass does "argue his formalist position more strenuously and inventively than most."[1] Bruss is right. Rather than adopting as his chief authorial imperative Ezra Pound's call to modernism—"make it new"—Gass follows a dictum from his elected soulmate, Rilke, who says, "Everything is gestation and then bringing forth. To let each impression and each germ of a feeling come to completion wholly in itself. . . , and await with deep humility and patience the birth-hour of a new clarity: that alone is living the artist's life: in understanding as in creating."[2] Gass's essays pursue not novelty but effulgence, the most complete gestation possible. They display his self-confessed "baroque sensibility."[3] In preference to imitating prairies, spare and level, renewed by fire, Gass's essays mimic old-growth forest, dense and lush.

Because they renounce novelty, Gass's essays change very little over time, remaining consistent both in style and in their preoccupations, a fixity Gass predicts in the preface to his first essay collection, *Fiction and the Figures of Life,* where he asserts a unity among the pieces assembled in it, in spite of their being composed individually and without regard for one another. "I don't believe I go back on my words very often," he says, "and I would suggest to any reader with the idleness and inclination to pursue it, that he will find shifts of emphasis, mainly, not basic alterations in ideas" (*FFL,* xii). That assertion might justifiably be extended beyond one book to all his essays, though they have been written over a period of more than forty years. In the fugal style Gass admires and often practices in his individual works of fiction, his essays collectively consist of variations on a set of repeated themes.

That fundamental unity diminishes the need to survey all of Gass's essays, despite their complexity and range. A few samples will illuminate Gass's approach to the essay, and verify the view that though there may have been small "shifts of emphasis," there have been no "basic alterations" in Gass's ideas. Bruss observes that "Gass's major theoretical concern is the *ontology* of literature. . . , the peculiar mode of being that distinguishes literary language, first, from material objects, and second, from any other kind of discourse" (140). That concern permeates Gass's essays, from the earliest to the most recent.

Consider, for example, the first essay, "Philosophy and the Form of Fiction," in his first collection, *Fiction and the Figures of Life*. For as long as philosophy has identified itself as a distinct enterprise, it has claimed a uniquely single-minded devotion to pursuit of the truth, as in the Greek distinction between *logos* (the sort of thing Plato claimed to be doing, and the word for which has given us English words like "dialogue" and "logical") and *mythos* (the sort of thing Homer and Sophocles had done, that Plato apparently considered dangerous, and the word for which is, obviously, the root of the English word "myth"). Philosophers, as the distinction might be made today, seek truth, and novelists tell stories without regard to truth. Gass begins by drawing that distinction into question, with the assertion that philosophers tell stories, too. Novels, he says, have nothing on philosophy when it comes to fiction. No "novelist has created a more

ONE THEME IN THREE ESSAYS

dashing hero than the handsome Absolute, or conceived more dramatic extrications—the soul's escape from the body, for instance, or the will's from cause" (*FFL,* 3).

Philosophy, Gass says, is fictional, and fiction philosophical. "Novelist and philosopher are both obsessed with language, and make themselves up out of concepts. Both, in a way, create worlds," and neither the philosophical world nor the fictional world is more real than the other. There are differences: philosophers attend more carefully to general nouns and verbs, while novelists "toil at filling in the blanks in proper names" (4); philosophy is an old practice, writing novels is comparatively new; philosophy, unlike fiction, has seldom understood that its concepts are metaphors and wish-fulfillments and myths; the philosopher "invites us to pass through his words to his subject," but the novelist keeps us "kindly imprisoned in his language" (8). Still, Gass says, though "they go about it in different ways," novelists and philosophers alike "are engaged in telling us *how it is*" (5). That commonality of purpose between philosopher and novelist brings Gass to his primary thesis: that "the esthetic aim of any fiction [philosophical or novelistic] is the creation of a verbal world, or a significant part of such a world, alive through every order of its being" (7).

Gass tries to do in regard to language what the philosopher Kant tried to do in regard to the mind in his *Critique of Pure Reason,* the aim of which he stated in this way: "Thus far it has been assumed that all our cognition must conform to objects. On that presupposition, however, all our attempts" to expand our cognition reliably "have come to nothing. Let us, therefore, try to find out by experiment whether we shall not make better progress in the problems of metaphysics if we assume that objects must conform to our cognition."[4]

Gass makes one modification to this Kantian purpose: instead of taking the categories of perception and understanding as cognitive and denying our access to the "thing in itself," as Kant argues, leaving objects only one option, to conform to our cognition, Gass makes the categories syntactic and lexical, and contends that the world must conform to our *words*. Gass's view still leaves no room for things in themselves: through language we construct ourselves, and through language we construct the world; language and we ourselves are "in" texts; we and the world are fictional, made not of the elements in the periodic table but of the words in the dictionary.

Aristotle, the prototypical philosopher, reasoned, according to Gass, "from the syntax of the Greek language to the syntax of reality," though he might not have recognized or been willing to admit that he was doing so. Gass says fiction reasons similarly, "since its people and their destinies, the things they prize, the way they feel, the landscapes they inhabit, are indistinct from words and all their orderings" (8). As a consequence, fiction has to meet a philosophical standard: it may not be philosophical, but the world it creates must be "philosophically adequate," a "different matter altogether" than creating "an adequate philosophy." To create a philosophically adequate world, the novelist creates a work complex and coherent enough that it would support a philosophical view based on or derived from it. In Gass's words, the novelist "creates an object, often as intricate and rigorous as any mathematic, often as simple and undemanding as a baby's toy, from whose nature, as from our own world, a philosophical system may be inferred; but he does not, except by inadvertance or mistaken esthetic principle, deem it his task to philosophize" (9).

Because the philosophical system is to be inferred, the worlds the writer creates "are only imaginatively possible ones; they need not

ONE THEME IN THREE ESSAYS

be at all like any real one" (9), including the one we live in, though they do need to be possible and internally consistent. Gass's choice of mathematics as a point of comparison supports his view, offering two particularly helpful analogies: first, in geometry, there are no "real" triangles or other Euclidean figures in the world we live in, yet triangles and other geometrical figures hold places in an imaginatively possible world that is a valid object of human attention. Second, the crucial element that makes the possible world of mathematics a valid object of human attention is form. The square of the hypotenuse on a right triangle equals the sum of the squares of the two short sides with a strictly formal necessity, containing no material or physical element. The Pythagorean theorem does not talk about the real world, but a hypothetical world: *if* there *were* a right triangle, then the square of its hypotenuse.... Similarly, the world of the fictional work, Gass argues, "displays that form of embodied thought which is imagination" (10), but does not replicate the "real world."

In creating fiction, the basic unit of the imagination, according to Gass, is the sentence. Sentences are "separate acts of creation," and "the most elementary instances of what the author has constructed" (12). They must "do more than simply configure things. Each should contrive (through order, meaning, sound, and rhythm) a moving unity of fact and feeling" (12). Here Gass relies most heavily on his formalism: through a formal quality (unity) of formal characteristics (order, sound, and rhythm), Gass thinks that a sentence "takes metaphysical dictation," and the accumulation of these dictations lends the work "its philosophical quality, and the form of life in the thing that has been made" (14).

Because the world of fiction need be only "imaginatively possible," the writer reserves the freedom to establish the "laws of nature" in that world. The rules "can be as many as the writer wishes, and they can be of any kind he wishes. They establish the logic, the order, of his world. They permit us to expect one event will follow another, or one sentence another, or one word another" (21). Instead of *describing* a world, the writer of a novel, in Gass's view, *constructs* a world.

The work's ability to create a world depends on language's ability to undergo ontological transformation, to become a different kind of thing in one use than in another. In "Carrots, Noses, Snow, Rose, Roses," Gass makes his case that such a transformation occurs in literature. He argues that "the words on checks and bills of lading, in guides and invoices" are not "in any central or essential sense the same as the passionately useless rigamarole that makes up literary language, because the words" in literature "have undergone a radical, though scarcely surprising, ontological transformation" (*WWW*, 283). Despite its radical nature, the transformation occurs through "such an unassuming process" that "it often passes unnoticed," like digestion (285). Whether observed or not, though, the transformation is complete: "the language of the poet or novelist is not the language of everyday" (284).

As if to illustrate Larry McCaffery's observation that Gass's essays do not "gloss, explicate, or 'argue' in the traditional sense," but instead use "striking similes and elaborate analogies and metaphors" to make their case,[5] "Carrots, Noses . . ." appropriates as its spine the metaphor of a snowman, which acts as "a lesson in ontology" because the various parts—snow rolled into balls, lumps of coal, a carrot, and so on—when arranged in the form of a snowman do not merely imitate but *become* parts of the snowman—his body and head, eyes, and nose, respectively. They undergo this ontological transformation not because they are "realistic" (the maker of the snowman

ONE THEME IN THREE ESSAYS

does not aim to "reproduce the shape of a man in snow," and the snowman looks very little like a human being), but because they follow a traditional form. That *form* brings about the trans*form*ation, "a fundamental alteration in the way a thing is" (293). To take one of the elements, the carrot, once positioned on the top snowball, "does not simply stand for or resemble a nose, *it literally is a nose now*—the nose of a specific snowman" (288).

The transformation does not occur because the carrot by itself looks any different than it did before, or because the individual words look or sound any different. "The cold unscraped carrot we planted above the snowman's mouth" still "resembles its former self perfectly, rooty all the way, just as the words of poems do." The change is strictly "internal" or "invisible," a change in being, not in seeming, "for poetry is not a process of acculturation, but a process of ontological transformation, and essences, not appearances, mere accidents and qualities, are involved" (294). The carrot retains its character as a carrot regardless of the rest of its context, whether growing underground, served steaming on a plate, or used in a comedy to conduct an orchestra, but its transformation into a nose depends on context utterly. The snowman's facial features are facial features only together: "as eyes and nose, they need each other; as carrot or coal, they couldn't care" (294).

Gass inserts one qualification that might not be apparent from the snowman metaphor, namely that "there are degrees and distances of ontological transformations" (289), a distinction necessary because language "moves toward poetry," and "becomes increasingly concrete," rather than being transformed instantaneously and absolutely. The gradual transformation from ordinary language to literature occurs through "denying the distinction between type and token, the sign and its significance, name and thing" (303). Language that does so "abandons its traditional semantic capacities in favor of increasingly contextual interaction. The words respond to one another as actors, dancers, do, and thus their so-called object is not rendered or described but constructed" (304). After assuming such a mutual (formal) relation, "language refuses all translation, becomes frozen in its formulas," because any alteration disturbs the relationship that establishes the ontology. Consequently, literary language, dependent as it is on the preservation of the interrelationships that transformed it, "invites, not use, not action, not consumption, but appreciation, contemplation, conservation, repetition, praise" (304). The snowman does not invite us to do something with him, or challenge us to do something because of him, only to pay him attention, and the same holds, Gass believes, for fiction.

In "The Book As a Container of Consciousness," the last essay in *Finding a Form,* Gass enumerates the six elements that he thinks account for the "containment of a consciousness" that happens when language has undergone the ontological transformation into literature.[6]

1. Perception: The first element occurs when the writer achieves a heightened awareness. "When a thing is seen, it says its name and begs to be perceived as fully and richly as possible"; such perception transforms the thing "into an item in consciousness" (345), available for containment in the text. The thing as a thing cannot be contained in language, Gass implies, but as a perception (an item in consciousness) it can.

2. Emotion: Because "experience is everywhere toned by our mood, soothed or inflamed by immediate feeling," and because "these emotions are modified by what we see or think

or imagine, so that sometimes new ones will emerge" (346), emotion cannot be isolated from perception, nor perception from emotion. The two stand in a mutual interrelationship that, like the interrelationship between the carrot and the lumps of coal, defines their ontological status. We see what we see, and we see the way we see, because of what we feel; and we feel what we feel because of how and what we see.

3. Thought: "Thought is another essential character in consciousness" that informs and checks the others. Without thought, perception and emotion cannot be trusted: a person may feel persecuted—or loved—and be deceived in the feeling, with no instrument for detecting the deception except for thought. Similarly, a person may perceive (in the standard example) a pencil in a glass of water as bent, and only know to distrust the perception because of thought.

4. Speech: The primary tool of thought, according to Gass, is speech, construed broadly enough to include talking to oneself. "For the most part," he says, "our formal thought goes on in words" (346). The other ingredients in consciousness (emotions, perceptions, and so on) find their order in and through sentences; consequently, the identity of the consciousness derives from those same sentences. "In order to be known, we speak. Even to ourselves" (347).

5. Desire: Desires have a simple function: to "put purpose in our behavior, position the body in the surf, urge us to overcome obstacles or make hay while the sun shines" (347). Desire defines what we consider good and what bad. Desire occurs in mutual interrelationship with the other elements: it needs

regulation by thought and formulation in speech, it influences emotion, and helps direct perception.

6. Imagination: As the sixth element in his recipe for consciousness, Gass identifies "what Coleridge called the esemplastic power—that of the creative imagination" (347). Functioning comparatively, the imagination works as "a model maker, bringing this and that together to see how different they are or how much the same" (347), a task on which the other elements depend: how could one desire, for instance, without the comparative act that is imagination?

As the essay draws toward its close, Gass introduces disclaimers such as the acknowledgment that "the consciousness contained in any text is not an actual functioning consciousness; it is a constructed one, improved, pared, paced, enriched by endless retrospection, irrelevancies removed" (348). Or, again, sentences are not actual stretches of human awareness but "little shimmied lengths of words *endeavoring to be* similar stretches of human awareness" (350, emphasis added). Backing down from the much stronger claims early in the book (language "is not the representation of thought . . . ; it is thought itself" [36]), these disclaimers reveal the weakness in Gass's theorizing, namely that he cannot decide whether literature is a consciousness metaphorically or actually. That inconsistency, though, does not prevent Gass from holding consistently that there is no nonlinguistic world for the novel to draw from, or be limited by, which contributes to the view expressed in the last sentence of *Finding a Form:* Gass's sense that art exists for its own sake.

In contrast to C. S. Lewis's supposition that "literature exists to teach what is useful, to honour what deserves honour, to appreciate what is delightful," and that "the useful, honorable, and delightful things are superior to it: it exists for their sake; its own use, honour, or delightfulness is derivative from theirs,"[7] Gass contends that, far from literature's being justified by other things or experiences, it is what justifies them. All objects and events, even "our tragic acts," are justified "when they prompt such lines" as those of Blake or Sir Thomas Browne or Yeats (352).

If Gass's argument that the world must conform to our words functions by analogy with Kant's argument that the world must conform to our cognition, Gass's version of "art for art's sake" operates by analogy with Kant's ethical theory, his "categorical imperative" that one should "act in such a way that you treat humanity" always "as an end, and never simply as a means."[8] Literature, because like human beings it has/is a consciousness, deserves, Gass says, the same respect due to human beings. Even if we use other human beings as a means through whom we learn about the world (for example), we ought to treat them as ends in themselves worthy of our attention and respect independently of their use-value; and the same holds for works of literature. His essays all rely on the underlying premise that "works of art are meant to be lived with and loved, and if we try to understand them, we should try to understand them as we try to understand anyone—in order to know *them* better, not in order to know something else" (*FFL,* 284).

CHAPTER FIVE

Two Shades of Blue: *Willie Masters' Lonesome Wife* and *On Being Blue*

In no other work does the story-like character of Gass's essays appear more plainly than in *On Being Blue,* nor the essay-like character of his fiction than in *Willie Masters' Lonesome Wife*. The former, an essay, seems in some ways more like a novel than does the latter, and the latter seems in some ways more like an essay than does the former. Of all Gass's books, *Willie Masters' Lonesome Wife* has been the most widely discussed and the most frequently written about, despite being Gass's weakest book; and *On Being Blue* has been the least widely discussed and the least frequently written about, though it is among his best and most popular books.

Gass himself confesses that *Willie Masters' Lonesome Wife* did not succeed as he had hoped. "I was trying out some things. Didn't work. Most of them didn't work," he admits. "I was trying to find a spatial coordinate to go with the music, but my ability to manipulate the spatial and visual side of the medium was so hopelessly amateurish . . . that the visual business was only occasionally successful." Continuing this line of thought, he eventually connects the book's failure to the degree to which it resembles an essay rather than fiction. "Too many of my ideas turned out to be only ideas—situations where the reader says: 'Oh, yeah, I get the idea,' but that's all there is to get, the idea." Which is not enough, because in fiction ideas "represent

TWO SHADES OF BLUE: *WILLIE MASTERS* AND *ON BEING BLUE*

inadequately embodied projects." A reader or a writer hungry for adequately embodied projects will "care only for affective effects."[1] *Willie Masters' Lonesome Wife* proved too exclusively an intellectual exercise, without enough emotional charge to sustain it.

Willie Masters' Lonesome Wife arises from Gass's distrust of conventional narrative form, which he thinks does not replicate reality in the way readers (and writers) often take for granted that it does. "Narration relies on the notions of event, cause, sequence, aim, and outcome," Gass observes; however, "none of these can be assumed to be an essential part of the nature of things. We find them only in accounts of a certain kind" (*FAF*, 239). In other words, we often mistake conventions of storytelling for features of the world. Having told stories in certain patterns for so long and with such consistency, we no longer recognize the patterns *as* patterns.

That particular aspect blindness leads us, in Gass's view, to neglect other narrative possibilities, leaving us subject to "nonfictitious nature," which now "has its way about a good deal. If in a story it rains, the streets usually get wet; if a man is stabbed, he bleeds; smoke can still be a sign of fire, and screams can be sounds of damsels in distress" (*FFL*, 23). But Gass allies himself with novelists who break those patterns: Laurence Sterne, Gertrude Stein, Italo Calvino, Julio Cortázar, and others. Predictably, he attempts to break those patterns himself, and nowhere does he try harder to do so than in *Willie Masters' Lonesome Wife*.

That ambition gives readers a clue about how to start understanding the book. "No novel is without its assumptions," Gass says, and it is "important to find them out, for they are not always the same assumptions the reader is ready, unconsciously, to make" (*FFL*, 23). In *Willie Masters' Lonesome Wife*, Gass employs a set of assumptions very different from the set of assumptions he expects the reader unconsciously to make, and apprehending the novel will occur only through distinguishing this particular novel's assumptions—the ones Gass *asks* the reader to make—from more typical assumptions—those Gass *expects* the reader to make. For this purpose, Gass's list of "notions" from the statement quoted above (event, cause, sequence, aim, outcome) offers a satisfactory heuristic, in accordance with Gass's declaration that "many fictions that appear to be experimental are actually demonstrations." He goes on to say that "in literature innovation that comes to something is nearly always formal. It is the expression of style at the level of narrative structure and fictional strategy."[2] *Willie Masters' Lonesome Wife,* which appears to be experimental fiction, supports a reading as an expression of style at the level of fictional strategy, specifically as an essay on event, cause, sequence, aim, and outcome.

Event. Instead of the book's events happening primarily to the characters, they happen primarily to the reader, in the form of "highly visual intrusions that systematically disrupt the textual givens of the moment." The prominence and the nature of the visual events in the book (nude photos, simulated coffee-cup stains, and so on) help maintain the author as a character distinct from Babs, who can come after her and supply the book with simulacra of items to which she refers, not in an effort to deceive the reader into accepting them as real coffee-cup stains, and therefore believing that Babs is real and trustworthy, but with an emphasis on their being fake, in order to remind the reader insistently that this is a fiction.

The visual events are "farcical presentation raised to its nth degree, maximalized of paratactics, generated by a clownish, arranging presence of indeterminate provenance."[3] For example, the text begins

TWO SHADES OF BLUE: *WILLIE MASTERS* AND *ON BEING BLUE*

as part of an image, a naked woman bending toward a block in her hand as if to eat it, and on the block the letter S. The image nods toward pornography by presenting a youthful, buxom woman in a suggestive pose, but then pulls back from and makes light of that association by posing the woman not with a human sexual partner but with a letter of the alphabet. Similarly, the book's opening evokes the tradition of illuminated manuscripts, in which painstakingly hand-copied sacred books begin with ornate images around the majuscule initial letter, but pokes fun at that tradition, too, by depicting not angels or virgins but the (very) worldly Babs. The "clownishness" of these visual events lends the book its tone.

Cause. One of the theoretical commitments that undergirds Gass's formalism, his belief that a fictional text possesses its own integrity, in no way dependent on the rest of the world for its being, is his view that causation in literature need not mimic causation in the world. "The nature of the novel," he says, "will not be understood at all until this is: *from any given body of fictional text, nothing necessarily follows, and anything plausibly may.* Authors," a category to which Gass devotes an essay in *Habitations of the Word,* "are gods—a little tinny sometimes but omnipotent no matter what, and plausible on top of that, if they can manage it" (*FFL,* 36).

In the world, an acorn cannot produce anything other than an oak; in a novel, an acorn might produce an oak, but it might produce a Steinway or a set of spurs instead. It can produce *anything* the writer wants it to. In *Willie Masters' Lonesome Wife,* the causation makes a show of defying patterns predictable from the world. At one point, a mock stage play shows a husband discovering a penis baked into his breakfast roll. His discovery causes not only the surprise we might expect it to cause, but also something that could not be predicted: a footnoted meditation on language and universals that begins by quoting John Locke. The clownishness of the visual events derives from their flaunting their implausibility, and that implausibility derives from their obviously fictional causation, from the tinniness of their author/god.

Sequence. Normally we construe sequence as events ordered by causation, but Gass's attempts to subvert standard ideas of event and cause entail an equally non-standard sequence. Gass puts the difference of sequence in terms of a preference for the internal over the external. "I haven't the dramatic imagination at all. Even my characters tend to turn away from one another and talk to the void. . . . The interactions which interest me tend to be interactions between parts of my own being."[4] In place of drama (events ordered by causation) he substitutes something like stream of consciousness, sequenced by internal dialogue between parts of a divided self. Gass's explanation certainly fits with his preference for character over plot, as highlighted in the preceding chapter, but nothing guarantees that he is right (or telling the truth) on this matter, and certainly others have seen different sequencing principles at work in *Willie Masters' Lonesome Wife*. Larry McCaffery, for example, argues that "the central orderings of the book are loosely based on the stages of sexual intercourse,"[5] with Babs's language mirroring the rise and fall of her excitement.

Watson L. Holloway observes a more subtle and complex (though not unrelated) ordering based on the arrangement of the different-colored signatures in the original edition.[6] The blue pages, he says, "suggest coolness, cerebration, and a more or less ordered remembrance of past events."[7] Within these blue pages are "three simultaneous sources of story, three concurrent voices, that are differentiated by roman, italic, and boldface type, respectively" (80). The first level, in italics, "is a third-person account of Babs's youthful sexual activity."

TWO SHADES OF BLUE: *WILLIE MASTERS* AND *ON BEING BLUE*

The second voice, "in roman letters, is from Babs's first-person point of view, the standard autobiographical mode." Finally, the voice in boldface makes "a kind of recurrent beat in the background, like a drone note" (81).

Like McCaffery, Holloway sees sexual excitement as part of the sequencing, arguing that as "the color of the pages changes into an oily olive, the paper becomes thicker and more highly textured, and the typography and graphic layout of the pages occasionally verge on outlandishness," the reader recognizes "Babs's rising level of coital excitement," and the text "varies wildly in form," producing "the illusion of undulation, of being on a roller coaster, of bouncing up and down—a sensation produced by selective distortion of letters" (82). The red section that follows the green section "continues in the hard-driving, three-part stream of thought that narrows into precise philosophical analysis of language" (83), and the concluding section, on white paper, "calls to mind formal reports and expensive publications. The prose is dignified and without gimmick, reflecting Babs's (postcoital) postreading sobriety and lack of erotic stimulation. Babs's mood is philosophical and her words are measured" (83–84).

Another sequencing principle in *Willie Masters' Lonesome Wife* is the mythic/archetypal juxtaposition familiar from founding texts of modernism, like T. S. Eliot's "The Waste Land." Such a principle would account for the multiple voices ("The Waste Land" was initially entitled "He Do the Police in Different Voices"), and for the book's parataxis, a characteristic common in modernist works. It would also suggest a continuity between *In the Heart of the Heart of the Country,* which employed frequent allusion to modernist masterpieces, and *Willie Masters' Lonesome Wife,* which makes use of some of the techniques they practiced.

Aim. Willie Masters' Lonesome Wife attempts to make the book a body. Through its various devices, it "gives body to textual activity" —or tries to. "The meanderings of the imagination and the material aspects of the writing figure there in the form of endless cross-references, textual drifts from one asterisk to another, circles left by the writer's coffee cup," and so on, as a result of which "the text takes body, becomes a body, while the body puts itself into words and expresses itself in the course of an alibi-narrative in which theme is strictly form(s)."[8]

Having argued in his essays that language undergoes an ontological change when it is shaped as literature (as snow does when it is shaped as a snowman), Gass tries in *Willie Masters' Lonesome Wife* to push language all the way through one ontological change (the change that makes it literature) and into another change (one that makes it a body).

Outcome. The outcome of *Willie Masters' Lonesome Wife* resembles the outcome of an essay. In Elizabeth Bruss's clear formulation, "Gass does take great care to avoid making any character a simple spokesman of 'the truth,'" but his fictional works "engage us principally as a competition of views that at its best is not so very different in kind from Gass's own beloved Platonic dialogues," and that resemblance leaves the reader "no alternative" but to read *Willie Masters' Lonesome Wife* as "dramatized philosophy, an ungainly allegory wherein Babs (the narrator) stands for language and Philip Gelvin (her unresponsive lover) stands for all the unimaginative and unfeeling readers and/or writers who misuse her."[9] As Plato makes Socrates (who wrote nothing that has been preserved and who according to Plato's own depiction vehemently opposed writing as a tool for philosophy) into the featured character in a number of written philosophical dialogues, so Gass makes Babs, whose explicit concern is sex, into the main character in a meditation on fiction.

Its radical questioning of event, cause, sequence, aim, and outcome makes *Willie Masters' Lonesome Wife* visibly distinct from Gass's other works, but not *entirely* different. It still uses devices familiar from Gass's other fiction, such as his penchant for giving special weight to the names of characters and the titles of books. Charles Caramello points out that the title "alludes not only to the romantic impulse" by echoing the name of Goethe's character Wilhelm Meister, and "to the idea of the pure poem," an idea championed by the poet Mallarmé, referred to as *le Maître,* but also, "more importantly, to Shakespeare," in literature the most masterful Willie of all, and certainly one Willie with a lonesome wife.[10] In the spirit of the book's identification of body and text, Willie Masters' lonesome wife bears the nickname "Babs," with its connection to body by sound association with "boobs," and its connection to language by sound association with "babble." There is also "wordplay on the husband's name (Will he master his lonesome wife?)," and "another wordplay based on the principal lover's name, Phil Gelvin: Will Phil fulfill her by filling her with Phil?"[11]

Still, its going farther than Gass's other fictional works in questioning traditional patterns of event, cause, sequence, aim, and outcome ultimately makes *Willie Masters' Lonesome Wife* weaker than his other work, not stronger. The problem with *Willie Masters' Lonesome Wife* is the general problem of metafiction: *if* fiction doesn't point to anything beyond itself, then *all* fiction is metafiction; if fiction *does* point beyond itself then metafiction isn't fiction, and isn't *about* fiction. *Willie Masters' Lonesome Wife* disregards E. M. Cioran's warning that "the writer must guard against reflecting obsessively upon language, must avoid making it the substance of his obsessions."[12] Self-reflection strengthens fiction unless, carried too far, as in *Willie Masters' Lonesome Wife,* it becomes an end in itself. "The self-consciousness of the enterprise, not in itself a bad thing, has preempted the work" so completely that "the shaping serves as an alternative to the words themselves, but the self-consciousness of the conception returns us, always, to the author, not to the wife."[13]

To put this critique in other terms, the success of *Willie Masters' Lonesome Wife* lies so exclusively in its questioning of event, cause, sequence, aim, and outcome, that the work has value only as a means to the end of questioning. Yet, like Kantian ethical theory, Gass's own formalist criticism values literary work only when it is also an end in itself, not only a means. Gass asks consistently for his work (and any other fiction) to be judged as an end in itself, but judged in those terms, *Willie Masters' Lonesome Wife* just doesn't work.

Not long after calling *Willie Masters' Lonesome Wife* "dramatized philosophy," Elizabeth W. Bruss calls *On Being Blue* "Gass's most ambitious and most thoroughly ambiguated piece of theoretical literature. It is in many ways the companion piece, the inverse and more successful double, of *Willie Masters' Lonesome Wife*." Both are "discourses on language"; specifically, each is "an inquiry into its nature, its relationship to human consciousness, to memory and imagination." Both, she says, "use sexuality and eroticism as the centerpiece for an attack on imaginative impoverishment and the crude or voyeuristic lust for copies—as opposed to constructions beloved for their own sake."[14] Both books rely heavy on modernist paratactic association and juxtaposition, rather than more "traditional" ordering principles. "My stories," Gass says, in a comment that applies well to *Willie Masters' Lonesome Wife,* "are malevolently anti-narrative, and

TWO SHADES OF BLUE: *WILLIE MASTERS* AND *ON BEING BLUE*

my essays," especially *On Being Blue,* "are maliciously anti-expository" (*FAF*, 46).

Gass's own description of *On Being Blue* assents to Bruss's description of it as a discourse on language, characterizing it specifically as a meditation on the accidents of etymology and usage. "In doing *On Being Blue,*" he says, "I was struck by the way in which meanings are historically attached to words: it is so accidental, so remote, so twisted. A word is like a schoolgirl's room—a complete mess—so the great thing is to make out a way of seeing it all as ordered, as right, as inferred and following."[15] *On Being Blue* shares some of Gass's idiosyncrasies. For instance, just as he claims in his fiction to be interested first and foremost in the *name* of the character, in *On Being Blue,* where blue is the main character, "the title and the word were what interested me, not the subject."[16]

The book begins with "an encyclopedic cetology of blue composed of various interpretations, instances, and uses of blue and blueness."[17] After that long, lush list of blue things (or, more exactly, of usages of the word *blue*), Gass borrows his first major metaphor—without saying so—from the presocratic philosopher Anaximenes, whose candidate for the arché, the first principle and substrate of the world, is air, which he says forms solid materials by condensation in a process like felting. Gass portrays the meanings of the word *blue* as having condensed out of language in that way: "a random set of meanings has softly gathered around the word the way lint collects. The mind does that. A single word, a single thought, a single thing, as Plato taught. We cover our concepts, like fish, with clouds of net" (7).

The felting metaphor brings out the tension between order and disorder in the meanings of words, and in the case of blue, that tension appears most clearly in the meanings that have to do with sexuality, because sexuality includes within itself such extremes of order and disorder. "Nowhere," Gass says, "do we need order more than at any orgy" (8). Sexuality in language draws the most attention from readers or auditors, and therefore receives the most attention from writers or speakers: "we always plate our sexual subjects first. It is the original reason why we read . . . the only reason why we write" (10). As sexuality can confuse identity, leading lover and beloved to absorb one another's selves, so in the case of blue "the word and the condition, the color and the act, contrive to contain one another, as if the bottle of the genii were its belly, the lamp's breath the smoke of the wraith" (11). *Blue* is blue, and blue is *blue*.

The second section tries to give an account of "the responsibilities owed to language by both reader and author,"[18] but it begins where the first section left off: with sex. That sexuality receives the most attention in literature does not mean that it deserves the most attention, Gass says, and *On Being Blue* suggests that the disproportionate attention given to sexuality serves as one indicator that fiction does not actually pursue realism in the way it often pretends. According to Gass, if an author "claims that reality requires his depiction of the sexual, in addition to having a misguided aesthetic, he is a liar, since we shall surely see how few of his precious passages are devoted to chewing cabbage, hand-washing, sneezing, sitting on the stool, or, if you prefer, filling out forms, washing floors, cheering teams" (16). As a result of that misguided aesthetic, "the sexual, in most works, disrupts the form; there is an almost immediate dishevelment, the proportion of events is lost" (16–17). Gass's own fiction, especially *The Tunnel,* can be read as an attempt to restore events to proper proportion.

TWO SHADES OF BLUE: *WILLIE MASTERS* AND *ON BEING BLUE*

Gass thinks that "words are properties of thoughts, and thoughts cannot be thought without them" (21), a corollary of Nietzsche's claim that "we always express our thoughts with the words that lie to hand," and "we have at any moment only the thought for which we have to hand the words."[19] So our use of "dirty" words and their relative plenitude compared to the relative dearth of other descriptive words about sex constitutes a critique of our stance toward, and understanding of, sexuality. Taking the "dirty" words themselves first, Gass asserts a whole set of difficulties with them: the first "is that there aren't nearly enough of them; the second is that the people who use them are normally numskulls and prudes; the third is that in general they're not at all sexy, and the main reason for this is that no one loves them enough" (24). He goes on, though, to make explicit the comparison between dirty words and the rest of our sexual vocabulary, lamenting that "we have more names for parts of horses than we have for kinds of kisses, and our earthy words are all . . . well . . . 'dirty,'" a fact that "says something dirty about us, no doubt, because in a society which had a mind for the body and other similarly vital things, there would be a word for coming down, or going up, words for nibbles on the bias, earlobe loving, and every variety of tongue track" (25). A richer vocabulary of "dirty" words would alter (and enrich) their function, removing their (and our) dirtiness.

Gass's real agenda comes out, though, in his enlarging this observation from the narrow domain of sexual vocabulary to the very broad domain of consciousness in general. "We have a name for the Second Coming but none for a second coming. In fact our entire vocabulary for states of consciousness is critically impoverished" (25). Enlarging the claim thus to states of consciousness supports his assertion that "the true sexuality in literature—sex as a positive aesthetic quality" (43), blueness at its best, occurs in the kind of consciousness unique to literature, after words have undergone the ontological transformation whose occurrence he alleges in his other essays.

Section III, in which "Gass introduces use, intention, and utterance and suggests their similarity to sentence, speech, and part of speech,"[20] gives the clearest clue to what Gass has many of his characters, above all Kohler in *The Tunnel,* do in his fiction: "when we swear we say we let off steam by throwing our words at someone or something. 'Fuck you,' I mutter to the backside of the traffic cop, though I am innocent of any such intention" (48). That simple example "allows us to separate what is meant from what is said, and what is said from what is implied, and what is implied from what is revealed" (48), and identifies those separations as the project for a reader of *The Tunnel:* what does Kohler mean, what does he say, what does he imply, and what does he reveal? As will become clear in the next chapter, the success or failure of *The Tunnel* depends on the distinction between meaning, implication, and revelation in Kohler's long rant.

The short final section "explores blue as a mode of perception and from there erects it as the ultimate ontology."[21] The perception and ontology resemble each other in being comparative: "just as *seeing* blue involves a comparison between longer and shorter wavelengths over the total visual field, *being* blue consists of a set of comparisons too" (81). Blueness creates a textual privacy out of the unidirectionality of words. Because "words are one-way mirrors" (84), we can employ them voyeuristically, and "books whose blueness penetrates the pages between their covers are books which, without depriving us of the comfort of our own commode or the sight of our liberal selves, place us inside a manufactured privacy" (84–85). As always, the central issue remains consciousness. Gass proposes that

TWO SHADES OF BLUE: *WILLIE MASTERS* AND *ON BEING BLUE*

blueness as consciousness operates like blueness in the sky, becoming clear as one approaches it. "Blue as you enter it disappears. Red never does that. Every article of air might look like cobalt if we got outside ourselves to see it. The country of the blue is clear" (86).

To borrow a final formulation from Melanie Eckford-Prossor, as a means of returning to the opening observation of this chapter, about the blurring of genres in *Willie Masters' Lonesome Wife* and *On Being Blue,* Gass tries in *On Being Blue* to affirm metaphor and "to deny the validity of genre."[22] Gass's attraction to "ideas as playthings" asserts itself in both books, which, by "wander[ing] around philosophy" create "a world where ideas are characters; they have histories, fates, and so on."[23] That *ideas* function as characters in *Willie Masters' Lonesome Wife* gives it more of the flavor of an essay than most novels have, and that ideas function as *characters* in *On Being Blue* gives it more of the flavor of a novel than most essays have. Both books draw attention to the central position ideas hold in all of Gass's work.

CHAPTER SIX

Twenty Questions on *The Tunnel*

William H. Gass has staked his current reputation and his claim to posterity on *The Tunnel,* clearly presenting it as his magnum opus. Having devoted thirty years to it, Gass consistently describes *The Tunnel* as central to his oeuvre when he talks or writes about his career. "All my work up to it," he says, "I have privately thought of as exercises and preparations."[1] The conscious desire to create a magnum opus stands among the explicit motivating factors behind the writing of *The Tunnel.* Gass says that the novelists he most admires from his own generation, including William Gaddis, John Barth, and Stanley Elkin, all held "the old romantic ambition of the Great American Novel,"[2] and that the writers he admires from earlier generations and from other countries, "whether they write long, big books or not, have that ambition of looking at their career as a life devoted to certain projects," specifically to writing "the great book."[3]

But staking his career on one book—especially *this* book—was a risky venture, and Gass's own definition of winning the bet reverses the standard view. Definitions of success for a book usually include some form of consensus, either popular consensus (the book becomes a bestseller) or critical consensus (favorable reviews in major periodicals, widespread use in classrooms, inclusion in "the canon"). Gass, though, not only predicts a lack of consensus for the book ("I can't imagine that most people will want to wade through it"[4]), but also, and more importantly, tries to *exclude* consensus as a criterion of the book's success, having stated more than once the seemingly paradoxical ambition that it be "such a good book no one will want to publish it."[5]

1. What have readers thought of the book?

Though apparently the book was not good enough to go unpublished, Gass predicted rightly that most people would not want to wade through it. Of those who *did* wade through it, enough wished they had not that no consensus has yet formed on whether the book succeeds. *The Tunnel* was widely reviewed, but early responses ranged from wildly enthusiastic to contemptuous. Michael Silverblatt's "A Small Apartment in Hell" represents the former extreme, and Robert Alter's "The Leveling Wind" represents the latter. Silverblatt begins his review by calling *The Tunnel* "the most beautiful, most complex, most disturbing novel to be published in my lifetime."[6] The book's beauty, complexity, and disturbance arise, according to Silverblatt, from the juxtaposition of its "annihilating sensibility" with the beauty of its language and its "stoic sympathy" in depicting "what we used to call the human condition" (12). Kohler, the book's main character, is a moral monster, Silverblatt says, but the book is terrifying because it enforces recognition of the extent to which Kohler "seems to be like us." Silverblatt concludes by describing the book itself in those terms, as "the most rigorously fearless moral inventory in all of literature" (13).

Robert Alter, in contrast, calls *The Tunnel* a "monster of a book" bloated by "sheer adipose verbosity and an unremitting condition of moral and intellectual flatulence."[7] Alter accuses Gass of having produced "a complete compendium of the vices of postmodern writing," beginning with the attempt to "disrupt the realist illusion." By filling Kohler's head, and (since it is the same thing) the novel's pages, with so many earlier books, "from Plato and Pascal to Kleist, Proust, and Rilke," Gass reduces everything to text. *The Tunnel,* according to Alter, also sins by its "transgression" of structural expectations. Instead of the linear narrative of traditional novels or the formal symmetries of modernist novels, *The Tunnel* offers only a "loose, unimpeded, free-associative flow" (30). Alter's list of vices continues with the narrator's unruliness, a lack of decorum that raises Alter's central criticism: that the removal of aesthetic distinctions (reflected in each of the vices) supports a leveling of moral values, and the novel itself attempts to "announce the end of moral history" (31), an attempt at which it fails because Kohler's cynical worldview overwhelms the novel, allowing "no glimpse of a complication or an alternative," and because the book trivializes genocide by equating it with "the nickel-and-dime nastiness that people perpetrate in everyday life" (32).

By adopting the imaginative procedure of putting the book on trial, and splitting himself for that purpose into prosecution and defense, Sven Birkerts captures, without attempting to mediate between, the opposite reactions that Silverblatt and Alter represent. The prosecution argues that *The Tunnel* is "a monster of skewed recollection," worrying certain details to death while neglecting "whole decades,"[8] and that *The Tunnel* does not cohere, does not "instruct or enlighten," and features a character with no redeeming value. The defense argues that the narrator *is* a horrific character, but that "we are being asked not to like him—Gass would be horrified if we did—but to *know* him" (117). According to the defense, the worrying of details takes the reader as close as possible to entering the mind of another person. And finally, the style accomplishes the goal Gass formulates in other books, to put a soul inside the sentence. Birkerts concludes that *The Tunnel* contains much to deplore and much to celebrate, "and I cannot see that either cancels the other" (120).

TWENTY QUESTIONS ON *THE TUNNEL*

To add to the many reviews, scholars began studying *The Tunnel* almost immediately. The first extended treatment of the book, a volume of essays entitled *Into "The Tunnel,"* edited by Steven G. Kellman and Irving Malin, contains an assortment of various short investigations (brief introductions, an interview, and topical essays) unified only by their attention to *The Tunnel* and by the conviction, stated by one of the editors, that *The Tunnel,* because it lacks a gist, "insists on multiple readings."[9] Such multivalence guarantees that, even within the first book about *The Tunnel,* in which the contributors appear to have been selected in part because they share the estimation *that* the novel is good, no consensus emerges as to *why* it is good.

In his essay, James McCourt reads *The Tunnel* as a performance of *Hamlet,* emphasizing "the closet scene and the graveyard scene" (21). McCourt affirms the rightness of the (non)action of the novel—that for 650 pages the protagonist does little other than sit in a chair or dig a tunnel—by suggesting that our lives look like Kohler's life: "the only available occupational resources *are* sitting in a chair talking and digging our own graves" (23). Though he sees the novel as a "requiem for a world that began ending in Dallas on 22 November 1963," McCourt attributes the book's power to Kohler's failure being universal, just like Ahab's in *Moby Dick,* and that universality makes his condition not political, but "primal."

Susan Stewart's "An American Faust" sees *The Tunnel* as the story of "the ethical relation between the individual and the collective in the twentieth century" (36), a "negative allegory of Hegel's lectures on reason in history" (38). Kohler presents us with experience "as a blow or wound"(39), making his history a history of trauma. Stewart observes that "the book does not produce catharsis; rather, catharsis produces the book" (41). She traces in *The Tunnel* the narrator's frustrated Freudian relationship to the body of the mother, and concludes by noting parallels between *The Tunnel* and the Faust myth, especially as exemplified by Thomas Mann's *Doktor Faustus:* for example, the presence of Magus Tabor as a Mephistopheles figure.

In "Is There Light at the End of *The Tunnel?*," Heide Ziegler contends that *The Tunnel* is not the formalist work one might expect from the staunchly formalist Gass, but "treads" instead on "moral ground." In the shadow of Kohler's *Guilt and Innocence in Hitler's Germany,* the distinction between guilt and innocence disappears. *"The Tunnel* is a descent into our collective unconscious, an expression of the underside, so to speak, of our *Zeitgeist"* (73). Ziegler observes that the tunnel "is Gass's metaphor, not Kohler's" (76), and serves therefore as the first distinction between the author and the narrator. She compares *The Tunnel* to Bunyan's *The Pilgrim's Progress,* noting that in each the reader is confronted with a series of vices, but that, in contrast to *The Pilgrim's Progress,* "no vice is ever overcome in *The Tunnel*" (79). Ziegler argues that Gass attempts "to change the Holocaust from a horrifying, unforgivable, yet singular European spectacle into a general historical possibility" (80).

The next extended response to *The Tunnel,* a web-based casebook posted by the *Review of Contemporary Fiction* on the website of the Center for Book Culture, offers views that are *more* disparate, not less.[10] Jonathan N. Barron considers *The Tunnel* profoundly challenging, and asserts that it "raises the question of genre and ethics by manipulating and crossing together" the techniques of fiction with those of "three truth-telling genres: autobiography, history, and poetry." Barron argues that "Gass creates genre confusion between fiction and these three discourse systems that claim to have a corner on the truth market." Fiction seems to cancel out the truth-telling genres, but Gass overcomes the cancellation by incorporating into *The Tunnel* a fourth truth-telling genre, lyric poetry, so that it "allows 'the actual' and 'the conceptual' to meet, to clash, and, in the resulting chaos of explosive contact to reveal, if only between the lines, the ethical, moral truths of our world outside of the book." Lyric poetry, Barron contends, redeems even the fascist Kohler.

In contrast to Barron's favorable assessment, Melanie Eckford-Prossor finds *The Tunnel* "intellectually intriguing" but also "ethically repugnant." She sees it as a novel that never finds a way to begin, a novel with "nowhere to go." Jim Barloon considers *The Tunnel* "gratuitously transgressive." *The Tunnel,* Barloon says, "in its deconstruction of language, history, the American family, is a little big novel, a text that reduces, like an e. e. cummings poem, traditionally large themes to lower-case status. While Nietzsche proclaimed, with *fin-de-siècle* bravura, the death of God, Gass (or Kohler) exclaims, in the spirit of a whoopee cushion, the death of whatever's left untoppled in the transcendental realm."

Debra Di Blasi considers *The Tunnel* not heroic in its innovation, but pretentious in claiming innovation for dated techniques. In fact, she proposes to replace Gass's PdP with a PdR, the Party of the Disappointed Reader, the reader who cannot suspend her disbelief in Kohler, the reader who concludes that "It's not really the excessive word play or illustrations or contradictory narrative voices I mind. What I mind is that when I finished the book, I didn't care" about Kohler or any of the characters, "except maybe Gass, because thirty years is a very long time out of a career, a life."

That readers' reactions to *The Tunnel* have been so widely, even wildly, various indicates that it may simply be too soon to expect anything like a consensus. Gass admits elsewhere that "we cannot say with certainty what [works] will live, and survival, by itself, is no guarantee of quality," but he immediately qualifies that statement by asserting that nevertheless, "we can say something about what is deserving."[11] So it is in regard to *The Tunnel:* no one can predict yet whether it will last, but that does not prevent the attempt to establish some terms for understanding and some conditions for assessing the book.

2. What was Gass trying to achieve in this book?

Of Gass's several clear statements of his intent in writing *The Tunnel,* each seems to contradict his often-repeated statement that "you don't write 'about' anything. That's the whole point."[12]

In one essay, Gass implies that the Holocaust serves as subject of *The Tunnel* because of the paradox it poses. If the Holocaust "remains inside the causal stream, it becomes just another pogrom, the largest so far, to be sure, but merely big, not otherwise special."[13] In other words, if the Holocaust occurred through cause and effect, then it differs from other persecutions throughout history only by its scale; if the Holocaust differs only quantitatively but not qualitatively from other persecutions, then it has no special connection either with Jewishness or with Germanness, so the guilt shifts "from the Germans as a national group to Man as a species." On the other hand, treating the Holocaust "as a sacred occurrence, like a miracle made by Satan," with "no conditions or causes, and certainly no historical consequences" (95), may seem to minimize blame, but it also means that if "there could be a Second Coming of this Catastrophe, we could never predict or prepare for it" (97), nor can we do anything to prevent its recurrence. "Let us bow our heads, for nothing can be done or said." Neither option allows us to exempt ourselves from the possibility of being in another holocaust, either as a perpetrator or as a victim.

TWENTY QUESTIONS ON *THE TUNNEL*

The Tunnel, then, tests this statement from the same essay: "If we come to the truth by comparing our descriptions of life with life itself, and by trying, then, to get our various versions to square, we arrive at our moral judgments through the narratives we fashion, during the composition of which various values simply make themselves manifest, with their positive and negative valences, their eventual weight and leverage" (77). When Kohler composes his self-indulgent and self-justifying narrative, what values will "make themselves manifest" to the reader: Kohler's? Gass's? the reader's own? If, as Gass apparently wants *The Tunnel* to imply, human nature is corrupt, then how and to whom will any but corrupt values make themselves manifest? How, in other words, could *The Tunnel* do anything except exacerbate human corruption? Even if uncorrupted values can manifest themselves to corrupt natures, nothing guarantees that comparing the two would be redemptive, and in fact Gass says it would not be. "Art does not," he contends, "have a hortatory influence; it's not a medicine, and it teaches nothing. It simply shows us what beauty, perfection, sensuality, and meaning are; and we feel as we should feel if we'd compared physiques with Hercules" (*FFL,* 274). Gass does not claim that *The Tunnel* teaches. According to his own statements, it cannot teach, and would not want to.

If *The Tunnel* does not delight *or* teach, the two traditional aims of literature named by Horace and echoed since, what *does* it do? One answer comes from an essay in which Gass compares architectural monuments to monumental literary works. Observing that, "in those modern American works of literature which aspire to the monumental," a category into which Gass wants *The Tunnel* to fit, "the past is not preserved or rescued . . . so much as it is broken up and dispersed."[14] Monumental works, he says, constitute "ordeals in the religious sense" that "weed out the unreliable, the unworthy" (140). Certainly *The Tunnel* constitutes an ordeal, if not in a religious sense at least in an aesthetic and ethical sense, and attempts like other ordeals to weed out the unworthy. As a purported instance of the monumental, it "is not easy to live with precisely because of what it so wholeheartedly demands: a life" (141). Like "Guernica" or the Vietnam Veterans Memorial in Washington, D.C., the monumental may attest to violence and evil, but in doing so demand a life that opposes what it records. If *The Tunnel* works, it mimics those monuments in demanding from the reader a mind opposed to the mind it monumentalizes.

In addition to making statements that can be related easily to *The Tunnel,* Gass has made explicit claims about his purposes in writing the book. "I hope to write about certain kinds of objectionable attitudes and feelings," he says, "in such a way that the reader will accept them, will have them, while he's reading. In that sense the book is a progressive indictment of the reader" that occurs not simply because Kohler has objectionable attitudes and feelings, but because he formulates them in such a way that the reader finds some attraction in them. "I want to get the reader to say yes to Kohler, although Kohler is a monster. That means that every reader in that moment has admitted to monstrousness. So my point of view in writing this book is less detached for me than normal."[15]

Lynne McFall provides a way of construing this purpose, a conceptual framework that helps explain how *The Tunnel* would succeed, if it did succeed, in fulfilling this aim. McFall distinguishes between first- and second-order preferences, giving as an example of a first-order preference her preference to smoke, and as an example of a second-order preference her preference to be the sort of person who prefers not to smoke.[16] She is divided; she wants to want not to smoke, but she doesn't

TWENTY QUESTIONS ON *THE TUNNEL*

want not to smoke. "One heart told me this, one heart told me that."[17] McFall's example shows that first- and second-order preferences that *appear* to contradict each other may not contradict each other at all. The second-order preference is really a preference for a possible world different from the actual world; within the actual world, though, the first-order preference reigns. Using this framework, one might say that Gass wants the reader of *The Tunnel* to recognize that, in spite of our second-order preference for the possible world in which we do not prefer the morally monstrous, we live in an actual world in which we do prefer the morally monstrous. We wish we were the sort of beings who do not prefer the morally monstrous, but we are not.

What McFall calls a second-order preference might be second-order through incoherence, as Gass says suicide is. "It doesn't follow at all that because it is easy enough to kill yourself, it is easy enough to get, in that case, what you want. Can you really be said to want what you cannot possibly understand? or what you are in abysmal confusion about? or what is proven contrary to your interests? or is plainly impossible?" (*WWW*, 6). The preference might be second-order through alignment with the repressed portion of a divided self, as occurs clearly in Frederick Seidel's "Descent into the Underworld," in which a female character says, "The man is bad—I hate him. / The little girl is bad. She loves him."[18] In such a case, one self, or one part of the self, maintains the first-order preference, and another self, or another part of the self, maintains the second-order preference.

In either case, giving voice to the second-order preference constructs an evil or untrustworthy narrator, whether with a flippant, ironic tone—as in E. J. Cullen's "I Break into Houses," where the narrator proposes as a foreign policy toward the Persian Gulf that, instead of "whip[ping] the camel-shit-eating bastards back into the deserts they came out of," we (Americans) should "steal the lames blind before they know what's what"[19]—or with a more serious, oppressive tone, as in *The Tunnel*. Gass's extending his despicable narrator's diatribe on his second-order preferences to 652 pages makes it clear that the book's ambition, formulated in its noblest terms, is "To say the most horrible thing such that it is no longer horrible; it gives one hope because it was said out loud."[20] The basest formulation of *The Tunnel*'s ambition can be extrapolated from this admission in one of Gass's essays: "It is an element in every author's impulse to speech and exposure: the desire to present the worst in oneself in the guise of a gift, as the child feels he has when he's used his pot" (*WWW*, 258). Kohler's preoccupation with feces symbolizes his will to tender the worst of himself, to present and display aspects of himself that social pressures lead most humans to try to hide.

3. Is *The Tunnel* a "postmodern" book?

In addition to asking what readers have seen in it and what Gass sought to accomplish, another preliminary toward understanding and assessing *The Tunnel* is to eliminate a red herring. One term frequently applied in assessments of *The Tunnel* is "postmodern." For instance, John Leonard calls *The Tunnel* a "panopticon of a postmodern novel that William Gass has been torturing for three decades, as Giacometti tortured metals."[21]

The consonance between the view of history Kohler espouses, in which words are more "real" than "real" things and events, with the deconstructionist mantra that "there is nothing outside the text" argues in favor of *The Tunnel*'s postmodernism, but ironically that consonance makes Gass's work hard to separate from a theoretical position he does not accept.[22] Gass's conviction that "among real things words win the gold medals for Being" (*FFL,* 48), though it leans toward the view that there is nothing extratextual, derives from his own staunch formalism, a decidedly modernist—*not* postmodernist—point of view.

Whether *The Tunnel* counts as "postmodern" or not depends on how one construes postmodernism. Jean-François Lyotard, for instance, describes it as (among other things) a resistance to the use of realism "to preserve various consciousnesses from doubt" and to "stabilize the referent, to arrange it according to a point of view which endows it with a recognizable meaning, to reproduce the syntax and vocabulary which enable the addressee to decipher images and sentences quickly, and so to arrive easily at the consciousness of his own identity as well as the approval which he thereby receives from others." The painter and the novelist "must question the rules of the art of painting or of narrative as they have learned and received them from their predecessors."[23] On that conception of postmodernism, *The Tunnel* is certainly postmodern, resisting as it does a "therapeutic" use.

On the other hand, Paul Mann treats postmodernism as "the death of the avant-garde," in which "everything verges toward exposure, publicity, the spectacle, interpretation and surveillance, and the surface of the screen."[24] On that conception of postmodernism, *The Tunnel* is definitely not postmodern, since it values concealment over exposure, privacy over publicity, consciousness over the spectacle, seclusion over surveillance, and depth over surface.

Whether *The Tunnel* is or is not postmodern may be a legitimate question, but answering it would help more in framing a doctrine of postmodernism than in interpreting or evaluating this novel.

4. What are some of the book's predecessors?

Some of *The Tunnel*'s sources, influences, and models are easy to identify. Dostoevsky's *Notes from Underground* and Kafka's "The Burrow," both by well-known and often-studied authors, are obvious candidates. Bernhard Kellerman's *Der Tunnel* (1913) "was crucial for me," Gass says, "because Kellerman's novel was the novel that was made into a movie which was Hitler's favorite." Also, "Dorothy Richardson, a woman who wrote a lot of long novels in the same period as Virginia Woolf, wrote *The Tunnel*."[25] In addition, Ernesto Sábato wrote a novel called *El túnel;* Gass has written about Sábato that his "position—as it seems from *my very different yet identical point of view*—is rather well put by Marcuse: 'The aesthetic necessity of art supersedes the terrible necessity of reality, sublimates its pain and pleasure; the blind suffering and cruelty of nature assume meaning and end—"poetic justice." ' "[26]

One might also look outside the realm of fiction, though, for less obvious but no less important antecedents. For instance, philosophy provides possible predecessors, as one might expect, given Gass's formal training as a philosopher. Thus, one reviewer's observation that Kohler sets out to "besmear with slime everything the reader conceivably may value,"[27] helps reveal *The Tunnel* as having descended from a philosophical ancestor, Cartesian skepticism. Descartes, unsatisfied with the ideas and alleged facts he had been taught by "the schoolmen," creates "a Method, by whose assistance it appears to me I have the means of gradually increasing my knowledge"[28] and ensuring the certainty of that knowledge, giving it a basis more secure than the authority on which the lessons he was taught in school were based. His method, in brief, doubts everything that can be doubted, thereby taking "all the opinions which up to

TWENTY QUESTIONS ON *THE TUNNEL*

this time I had embraced," and "sweep[ing] them completely away" (89), using the indubitable residue (which he identifies with the famous formulation "I think, therefore I am") as the foundation for certain knowledge. Descartes categorizes his *Discourse on Method* not as a philosophical treatise, but in terms that resemble those of *The Tunnel:* autobiography ("I shall be very happy to show the paths I have followed, and to set forth my life as in a picture" [83]) and history (advising his readers to view it "simply as a history" (83) that narrates a series of events but does not bind the reader to a given response).

One might understand *The Tunnel,* then, as a translation of the Cartesian project from epistemology (the study of knowledge, in which Descartes tries to solve the question of certainty and what grounds certainty) to ethics (in which Kohler raises the question of morality/virtue and what grounds morality/virtue). Descartes tries to doubt everything that can be doubted as a means of identifying what is indubitable; Gass sets Kohler to devaluing everything, to see what cannot be devalued.

Reading *The Tunnel* against the background of Descartes' *Discourse on Method* anticipates question 7, below, "Is Kohler really William Gass?" by attributing to Gass an intention distinct from the intention attributed to Kohler, treating *The Tunnel* as a case of satirical schizoscription, in which the proxy (the reader's construct of William Gass) opposes the narrator (the reader's construct of William Kohler).[29] Descartes was not, as some of his contemporaries accused him of being, a skeptic; whether or not he succeeded at his aim, he tried to use a skeptical mindset as a *means* toward greater certainty and broader knowledge. Taking Descartes as a predecessor of *The Tunnel* leads the reader to view it similarly, reading Gass—again, whether or not he succeeds at his aim—as trying to use Kohler's nihilistic mindset as a means toward an affirmation of moral value.

Gass's lifelong interest in poetry encourages seeking precedents there as well. Gass has emphasized repeatedly how importantly poetry has influenced his work in general, citing especially the work of two poets, Paul Valéry and Rainer Maria Rilke. As regards *The Tunnel,* Rilke's *The Notebooks of Malte Laurids Brigge* is especially important, since it shares with *The Tunnel* characteristics like the titular alter ego, and since Gass has written about it that there is no book "I would have wished more fervently to have written than this intensely personal poem in prose, this profound meditation on seeing and reading."[30] One might also find poetic antecedents, though, among poets Gass seldom mentions and does not himself identify as such. Robert Browning, for instance, often employs the dramatic monologue in the voice of an amoral or immoral character. In that regard, "Caliban Upon Setebos," "My Last Duchess," or "Porphyria's Lover" help to clear the path *The Tunnel* will follow.

Poetry also serves as an antecedent of *The Tunnel* in another way. Although Gass has asserted that he wanted *The Tunnel* to be the ultimate anti-novel, to disprove a received view about what the novel is, and thereby to open up new possibilities for the genre, he does not achieve that goal, for reasons given in question 20 ("Is *The Tunnel* a 'great book'?") below. One might reframe the ambition, though, in a way that more accurately describes the way *The Tunnel* actually turned out, by saying that *The Tunnel* tries to disprove Edgar Allan Poe's argument that there can be no long poem. Poe contends that a poem must be short enough to be read in one sitting, and that, "what we term a long poem is, in fact, merely a succession of brief ones."[31] Excessive length, on Poe's view, deprives the poem of both intensity and unity of effect, on both of which poetry depends absolutely. *The Tunnel* seeks to be a long poem in prose (a category Gass sees as valuable, as in the passage quoted in the preceding paragraph), and to overcome both limitations. Intensity Gass pursues at the level of the sentence, according to his expressed ideal that "a badly made sentence is a judgment pronounced upon its perpetrator, and even one poor paragraph indelibly stains the soul" (*FAF,* 52). Unity of effect Gass pursues through the book's structure.

5. How is the book structured?

In a manuscript synopsis, Gass describes *The Tunnel* as a novel "in twelve Philippics." That the book's parts take the form of denunciatory speeches—rather than, for instance, incidents or episodes—indicates that the narrator's frame of mind will center the book's ambitions; around that axis revolve the otherwise not always clearly allied units of the book. Gass wants the book's division into twelve sections to allude to the twelve-tone musical scale, though his having maintained and expressed such an intention does not entail that a reader who explored *The Tunnel* without making that association would suffer.

The Tunnel, Gass says, is "organized in terms of two coordinates, one being the temporal coordinate that music offers, in particular the twelve-tone system. The book is divided into twelve sections, and each section has a fundamental theme." The themes are interwoven with varying emphasis, and "there is a kind of recombination all the time of the basic twelve tones, just like variations on a theme."[32] The book's sections themselves vary in form, but the most visibly "structured" sections, like the overall structure, also employ musical models. For example, the "Planmantee Particularly" chapters in the philippic on

"The Curse of Colleagues" employ a structure reminiscent of musical variations, and one of the chapters in the "Mad Meg" philippic borrows its title from the musical model it follows, "A Fugue."

Though the novel is structured as a series of harangues rather than of episodes, some events do get recounted. As if to corroborate Antonio Porchia's observation that "Out of a hundred years a few minutes were made that stayed with me, not a hundred years,"[33] Kohler fixates on only a few events out of his fifty years. Among those to which Kohler devotes attention are: a wreck that occurs on one of the family's Sunday drives during his youth, and in which someone in another car is killed; an incident on a family vacation, in which his mother believes she has left her wedding ring at a hotel some distance back, only to discover it safely in her suitcase; his own being overwhelmed as a child by a swarm of grasshoppers; his getting caught stealing pennies from his parents to satisfy his appetite for store-bought sweets; his having to have his foreskin peeled back by a doctor after he had too long neglected to keep it clean; his alcoholic mother's attempt to throw him a birthday party, which she botches by forgetting to mail the invitations; a severe storm during which a window shatters near his mother, leaving bits of glass in her hair; committing his mother to the hospital; his crawling into a heating duct one day at work; killing his wife's cat. The incidents do not explain one another as interdependent nodes in a temporal sequence with one leading to another in a causal chain, as they would in a plot; they explain (only) Kohler. Or, in terms more like Gass's own, *The Tunnel* is not structured to tell the story of Kohler's life, but to reveal his consciousness.

All the events are described from within Kohler; the book purports to be his thoughts, a record—a stream—of his consciousness. That fact about structure relates to theme in a manner one of Iris Murdoch's observations illuminates. Murdoch says that "streams of consciousness in fiction are usually moral indicators. The deepest thoughts and feelings of the fictional character are revealed, from *this* evidence he cannot escape!"[34] Stream of consciousness fulfills, in other words, the function of a polygraph: Kohler rambles so long he indicts himself.

Murdoch borrows Gilbert Ryle's distinction between "chronicles" and "histories," alleging that "if we consider a period of time during which we have been 'brooding' or 'thinking' we may attempt a description in the form of a moment-to-moment chronicle of introspectible events, such as images, or words uttered to oneself. Even when one is trying to think carefully and consecutively the 'inward stream' may contain, or be interrupted by, chance items, such as perceptions suddenly illuminated by irrelevant significance" (266). Kohler's inward stream gets interrupted in this way quite often, and the best way of describing the book's point in structural terms would be to say that Kohler cannot sustain chronicle and history as separate categories. He has written a history (*Guilt and Innocence in Hitler's Germany*), but his attempt to introduce the history take the form of chronicle; and even within the chronicle he keeps mistaking one genre for the other.

Immediately after identifying music as one structural coordinate for the book, Gass identifies the other primary coordinate as "the conception of the book as a tunnel itself. The writing of it, and the reader's experience of it, are tunnel-like. Presumably, the reader is passing through the text the way the narrator who is digging the tunnel is digging through the past; his past, our past."[35] The musical structure is temporal, and the tunnel structure metaphorical.

6. Why a tunnel?

Metaphors pervade the book, but two metaphors preside: the window and the tunnel. Gass signals the importance of windows by the title of one of the sections, but uses the title of the whole book to signal the importance of tunnels. Like windows, tunnels had appeared as metaphors in earlier fiction by Gass; for example, in "The Pedersen Kid," where Hans and Pa try to dig a tunnel through the snow to get to the barn without being seen. In *The Tunnel,* Kohler's tunnel fixation is general enough that he tells of unscrewing a metal plate on the wall of an office at the university, and entering "a passage filled with cobweb and pipe" that led to the maintenance tunnels; but the book's most important tunnel, of course, is the one Kohler devotes himself to digging in (or out of) the basement of his house.

As a metaphor, the tunnel is overdetermined: it is the dust/clay that represents human mortality; it is the great vagina that represents sexuality and the feminine, especially in this case the dangerous, masculinity-consuming feminine that Kohler so fears; it is a hole that exists precisely where and because there is nothing, so that it represents the paradoxes of being and nothingness. When Kohler imagines Martha catching him digging, he constructs explanations like, "you see here an historian hunting for a false cause, for a reason why I'm here which will not be the reason I'm here," or, "I am down here, my dear, looking for a reason to be down here" (148). Although the sexual aspect of the metaphor is occasionally explicit ("Ah, Martha, . . . I have my own hole now, your cunt is not the only cave" [462]), more often the tunnel and *The Tunnel* seem to be identified in Kohler's mind, as when he says what could refer to either or both, "I shall descend and bend, creating a whole . . . twelve philippics deep" (153). So heavily overdetermined a metaphor can and does reappear in numerous guises, enough to prompt Michael Dirda to ask, "How many different kinds of tunnel—womb, tomb, excretory tract, closet, trunk, even the name

TWENTY QUESTIONS ON *THE TUNNEL*

Gass (alley in German)—can one spot in these 650 often close and claustrophobic pages?"[36]

The tunnel gives Kohler a metaphor for Being, but it also gives Gass a metaphor around which to structure the book. When he talks about the book, Gass envisions the tunnel as its "tropological form": "The text must be, at one and the same time, a hollow, the emptiness which defines the hole; the removed dirt, which the narrator needs to conceal, i.e. a dispersed heap; and the structure, bed boards, etc. which are used to prop the tunnel up." The text, he thinks, must not only make use of a tunnel or be about a tunnel; it "must have the metaphorical shape of a tunnel, with a concealed opening, a drop, passages which move easily, those which narrow, points of collapse, etc."[37] Gass tries to make the book itself as tunnel-like as he can.

That the tunnel's being derives from its non-being gives Kohler a way to find meaning in manifest absurdity, to act in the face of what he often labels "disappointment." "A plaque on the front door may one day read: Herein lies a pointless passage put down by a Pretender to the Throne of Darkness. Let God uproot this pathway if He likes, we shall still stare at the hole the hole has left, and wonder at the works of Man, and marvel at the little bit that mostly *Is,* and at the awkward lot that mostly *Aint*" (153). Digging the tunnel makes Kohler the representative disappointed person, motivated by resentment but committed on an ongoing basis to an ineffective response. "With my tunnel I have committed the ultimate inactive act" (468).

In its preoccupation with the tunnel, Gass's book reverses the Orpheus and Eurydice story. Instead of William (Orpheus) drawing Martha (Eurydice) up to the light, she wills him back down into the underworld. In the older story, after Eurydice's untimely death by snakebite, Orpheus goes down into the underworld himself and, by charming the presiding gods with his singing, receives permission for his beloved wife to return to earth, on condition that he not look back at her as she follows him on the climb out. He could not resist, though, and "eager to see her, / Looked back in love, and she was gone."[38] In *The Tunnel,* the elements are inverted. The husband, Kohler, inhabits the underworld; he is there not because he died, but through his own volition; he turns to look at his wife out of loathing and fear rather than love; he wants not to be reunited with her but to escape her. By thus reversing the familiar story of beautiful song and incorruptible, tragic love, *The Tunnel* emphasizes its status as an allegory of poetry and love already corrupted, creating a hell on earth from which the underworld could only provide an escape.

The Tunnel also reverses another familiar ancient mythos, Plato's allegory of the cave. In *The Republic,* Socrates leads his interlocutors to imagine an underground cave in which some people have been bound since birth in a fixed position, able only to look at the wall opposite them, not at themselves or one another. Above and behind them stands a low wall and behind it a fire burns. People pass between the fire and the wall, "carrying all kinds of artifacts that project above it—statues of people and other animals,"[39] and so on. Light from the fire projects the shadows of these artifacts onto the wall the prisoners face. Because they can see nothing else, the prisoners assume the shadows themselves are real and animate, and attribute to the shadows the sounds they hear.

Socrates infers that, were one of the bound individuals to be "freed and suddenly compelled to stand up, turn his head, walk, and look up toward the light, he'd be pained and dazzled and unable to see the things whose shadows he'd seen before," he would mistakenly "believe that the things he saw earlier," the shadows, "were truer than the ones he was now being shown." If he were made to look at the light itself, his eyes would hurt, and he would "turn around and flee towards the things he's able to see." If he were forced even further, up the tunnel out into sunlight, he would resist, and, with eyes accustomed to the dim light of the cave, he would be "unable to see a single one of the things now said to be true." At first he would be able to see better by night and able only to look at shadows during the day, but eventually his eyes would adjust to the light of the sun.

Gass inverts the elements of the narrative. Plato's parable asserts the value of education (a word whose Latin root means to lead out or lead up), but *The Tunnel,* instead of showing a prisoner being freed and enlightened, shows Kohler reversing the path Plato advocates: he goes away from the light, down into the cave, affiliating himself metaphorically with darkness and deception and evil in preference to light and wisdom and good. Kohler subverts Socrates' expectation that anyone who has seen both will prefer light to darkness, so Gass's tunnel serves, in addition to its other purposes, as a way of contesting Socrates' view about the innate goodness of humans. Socrates holds that all humans will the good, and only ignorance leads a person to do ill, but *The Tunnel* depicts a non-ignorant character who wills evil, and suggests that this character represents all of humanity.

7. Who is Kohler?

The book's narrator, William Frederick Kohler, teaches German history at an unnamed university in Indiana. A specialist in the Nazi era, he is the author of *Nuremberg Notes,* a book that, because of its sympathetic view of those on trial for war crimes, earned him some notoriety when it was published. He has since completed the manuscript of his magnum opus, *Guilt and Innocence in Hitler's Germany,* on which he worked for many years. When he starts to write the preface, though, he finds himself suffering writer's block, and begins writing the confessional memoir that becomes *The Tunnel*. To hide it from his wife, he interleaves its pages between the pages of the manuscript of *Guilt and Innocence,* the place where he feels most confident she will not see it. Also, he begins digging a tunnel (or at least *says* he is digging a tunnel) under the basement of their house.

Gass manifests once again his penchant for choosing "loaded" names. "Kohle" in German means "coal," making Kohler an appropriate name for a person who is engaged—absurdly—in digging a tunnel out of his own basement and who "cinders everything."[40] Despite his name, though, "there is nothing genuinely German" about Kohler (18), as he himself admits: he was neither born nor raised in Germany; he lived there only for a short time as a student; and he learned German as a second language. So an alternative etymology serves as well: "kohl" is also a transliterated Arabic word that names a material, usually finely powdered antimony, used in the Orient to darken the eyelids, so a "kohler" is one who (metaphorically) darkens eyes. Such an overdetermination of "Kohler" fits Gass's preoccupation with names, and the pun on "antimony" and "antinomy" makes Kohler a degraded Kant, who instead of using the antinomy in pursuit of light uses it in pursuit of darkness. The name contains other resonances as well, from the sublime (the *Philosophical Investigations* of Ludwig Wittgenstein, the great philosopher who was at Cornell while Gass was there in graduate school, urges the reader, in a section on seeing figures first as one thing then as another, to consider "Köhler's figure of the interpenetrating hexagons,"[41] which in this context might

TWENTY QUESTIONS ON *THE TUNNEL*

be seen as an anticipation of Kohler's twelve philippics) to the ridiculous (a line of plumbing fixtures uses the brand name Kohler, a fact pointed out in the novel).

Kohler, like several other characters in Gass's fiction, is preoccupied with, and paranoid about, his diminutive penis, the size of which constantly reminds him of his frustrated sexuality, but also arises as the first point of his identification with Hitler: "I hated having a small cock, the bad jokes of small boys upon that point. I hated having a round face like a fat doll. Hitler hated being ordered around" (19). Frustrated sexuality itself stands for Kohler's various disappointments: his lackluster career, his failed marriage, his personal isolation, and so on.

Certainly Gass portrays Kohler as a bitter, petty man, with no obvious redeeming qualities. Apparently Gass does not *want* readers to find many redeeming qualities in Kohler; that seems part of the point of the book. Yet, personalities, even fictional ones, are complex, and a reader who looks long enough can find virtues even in Kohler, as Philip Graham does when he notes that "what Kohler has left unspoken about his professional perspective in [his two history books] is that he feels implicated in the very history of which he writes."[42] Viewed in those terms, Kohler becomes *better* than most of us, because his sense of responsibility exceeds our own. Too absolute an identification with the victims of crimes rather than the perpetrators may express a noble sentiment, but it also self-deceptively denies one's humanity, and falsely assesses one's motives as incorruptible. Kohler at least mimics, even if he does not quite fulfill, Simone Weil's ambitious ethical/spiritual ideal: "To be innocent is to bear the weight of the entire universe. It is to throw away the counterweight."[43]

Still, that generous discovery of a good side to Kohler hardly reflects the main current of his character, which might be described more aptly by contrasting him with Sisyphus, the Greek mythological figure who became a type of the existential hero in the writings of Albert Camus. In Sisyphus' endless labor of pushing a stone up a hill, Camus sees "that unspeakable penalty in which the whole being is exerted toward accomplishing nothing," and in his return to the bottom to start again, the occasion for a consciousness that elevates Sisyphus, making him superior to his fate. "That hour like a breathing-space which returns as surely as his suffering, that is the hour of consciousness. . . . The lucidity that was to constitute his torture at the same time crowns his victory. There is no fate that cannot be surmounted by scorn."[44] In Camus' Sisyphus, the metaphor speaks of elevation: Sisyphus pushes the boulder up to the heights, and the consciousness that his efforts produce ennobles him and indemnifies him against harm. In Gass's Kohler, consciousness remains the issue: he asks, ". . . is it truly the truth I want? What *do* I want? to find out who I am? What is the good of that?" (106), and laments that "anything you do gets you deeper in deeper in deeper in" (379); but Kohler's metaphor is one of descent rather than ascent: he digs down into the depths, and the consciousness displayed in the narration of that effort debases him and capitulates to harm already done. Sisyphus, ennobled by his defiant exertion of will, lives up to Kierkegaard's ideal that "I can die but I must not become tired. For what is it to have spirit but to have will, and what is it to have will but to have it beyond all measure, since the person who does not have it beyond all measure but only to a certain degree does not have it at all."[45] Unlike Sisyphus, Kohler, debased by his velleities, has lost his will and accepted, even embraced, disappointment.

8. Is Kohler really William Gass?

The fictional life of William Kohler shares several features with the real life of William Gass. The book portrays Kohler as a middle-aged professor of history at a midwestern university, writing in 1967; Gass, who was roughly Kohler's age at the time in which the book is set, and who began writing *The Tunnel* in the mid-1960s, spent his career as a professor of philosophy at midwestern universities. Kohler endured a difficult childhood with an alcoholic mother and an arthritic father, as did Gass. Kohler claims to have given up poetry for history in his youth, but retains a fascination with figures like Rilke; Gass claims to have given up poetry for fiction in his youth, and his lifelong fascination with Rilke culminated in a book of translation and commentary called *Reading Rilke*. Kohler devoted the best years of his career to writing his magnum opus, *Guilt and Innocence in Hitler's Germany;* Gass devoted the best years of *his* career to his own magnum opus, *The Tunnel*. And so on.

Its containing autobiographical elements does not, however, make *The Tunnel* straightforwardly autobiographical. Indeed, to identify Kohler's frame of mind too easily with Gass's would be not only to disregard Gass's stated intention to *construct*—not to reproduce—a consciousness in his fiction, but also to minimize those points of identity with the reader's own consciousness on which the book's force depends. If the book succeeds, Kohler *does* stand for William Gass, but not any more than he stands for you and me, and to enforce too strict an identity between the author and narrator—to insist (in other words) that *The Tunnel* is about its author's life—would be to repress the book's insistence that it is about the reader's life as well. As part of a judgment that the book fails,[46] one might *argue* for the identification of author and narrator, but to *assume* the identification would be naive.

As Robert Kelly observes, any author who adopts a satirical point of view, as Gass does by "creating such a sexist, bigoted, hate-filled character" and asking "the reader to accept his vision of the real," runs the risk of "being believed, taken literally," the way we still "tend to think Jonathan Swift loathed humankind on the strength of Gulliver's aversion."[47] Many of *The Tunnel*'s early readers recognized this distinction between author and narrator as a crux of the book, noting that "readers will naturally look for a way to distinguish Gass himself from the petty, self-absorbed, and deeply unpleasant narrator he has created," but that "they will find this extremely difficult to do."[48]

Not all readers have accomplished the task. Robert Alter, for instance, recognizes the need to distinguish "a complication or an alternative" to "the leveling, despairing, cynical, resentful worldview of William Kohler," and he expects Gass, "presumably committed to humane, democratic values," to be audible at all times over Kohler's grumbling, whispering its flaws into the reader's ear.[49] But Alter does not recognize the reader's obligation to participate in evaluating Kohler's leveling worldview, so he falls into the trap Kelly predicts some readers will, of assuming "complicity between author and protagonist." As a result, Alter can affirm "humane, democratic values" in the face of Kohler's nihilistic ramblings only by rejecting the book altogether.

Gass does not help matters, though, when, in response to his prediction that "unfriendly reviewers" will "delight in the opportunity to clothe me in Kohler's rags," he distances himself too completely from Kohler with claims like "I do not belong in Kohler's camp."[50] Although Kohler is not *only* or even *primarily* Gass (that is to say,

Gass and nobody else), if the book works, Kohler *is* Gass (that is to say, Gass and everybody else). When Gass denies being Kohler, he either oversimplifies to prevent the reader's refusing responsibility by adopting the Gass-and-nobody-else identification, or he fails just like any other reader who represses identification with Kohler. For Kohler to be everyman, he cannot be only Gass and not inept reviewers; but he also cannot be only inept reviewers and not Gass.

9. Who were Kohler's parents?

In the novel, Kohler is the only child of Frederick Karl Kohler and Margaret Phelps Finney Kohler, about whom we are given information no more reliable than any other information in the book and certainly no less tied to Kohler's own preoccupations and point of view. Kohler blames his parents for his own vices, claiming to have learned "bigotry and bitterness," along with "how to be a failure," from his father, and to have caught "a case of cowardice from my mother" (136).

His father loves baseball and "'the Sunday drive': late afternoon excursions to check on the progress of spring, the building of a road, the extent of flooding or wind damage, the color of leaves across the state line" (220). But those two seemingly benign pastimes cannot mask the small-mindedness that Kohler sees as his father's most distinctive character trait. Even in regard to so apparently generous a practice as the Sunday drive with the family, Kohler emphasizes how unnecessarily autocratic his father was, never allowing anyone else in the family to "choose the moment or suggest the route." Rather than serving as a family bonding ritual, the drive was a "princely habit" Kohler resented then and still resents, even in middle age and after having children of his own: "He couldn't just take the Chevy out by himself; he had to have his entourage; he had to drive more than the car" (222). Kohler feels he was displaced in his father's affections by the cars. "Our journeys," he says, "were for the sake of the Chevrolets and the black Packard" (508).

Physically, Kohler's father suffers from debilitating arthritis, and the distance between father and son manifests itself in the son's lack of interest in learning to drive as the father's worsening arthritis impedes his ability to drive. "My father felt obliged to make a man of me. What else were fathers for? And that meant teaching me to drive a car" (518). But even though the car has an automatic transmission (a capitulation to the father's arthritis), young Billy Kohler cannot manage even to back the car out of the driveway, and he runs over a forsythia bush in the yard. His father takes Billy's ineptitude personally, and keeps asking "the outcry question" that "might have been my name": "What is the matter with you?" (519). Frederick dismisses Billy completely; the last words attributed to his father in the section on learning to drive are, "what a kid, he ain't mine" (523).

Even though the elder Kohler does not succeed in teaching the younger to drive, the younger "did learn from my father how to be a bigot," a skill to which he was more attentive and for which he demonstrates far greater aptitude. His admission that he has become a bigot like his father transforms his description of his father's bigotry into a form of self-disclosure. According to Kohler's (self-) description, bigots, unlike racists, direct their venom against particular persons, not against "abstract universals." They feel that they have "been treated unfairly, not in a single transaction, but in the fundamental opportunities and course" of their lives (529). Bigots believe that the social contract has been broken; society has not held up its end of the bargain with them. The bigot, Kohler says, savors his hatred: "it is ultimately all he loves, all he cares for, all he tends" (530). Bigots, preoccupied as they are with "what has been taken away, removed without recompense," form "the backbone of the Party of the Disappointed People."

Kohler's father's debilitation results from arthritis, his mother's from severe alcoholism. Her condition manifests itself in various ways, including hoarding bottles (a behavior pattern also emphasized in "The Pedersen Kid," there as a trait of Jorge's father) and hoarding the money to buy more bottles. Since she is in no condition to leave the house to get more liquor, she resorts to having an affair with the man who delivers bread to their home, who gives her gin in exchange for sex, a situation Billy hates but does nothing to stop because, he reasons, she needs her addiction "not to survive, but to endure survival" (622). Kohler recalls his mother only with shame, and the affair becomes compressed into part of a sentence: "the time my mother fell on her water-laden rump going to answer the door, in a nervous hurry because she believed it might be the breadman with her booze" (485). Eventually, Kohler has to accompany her in a cab (having failed his father's driving lesson) to the asylum and have her committed, but not until she is in such bad shape that, when Kohler calls to have his father taken to the hospital, the ambulance attendants begin mistakenly to take her, and have to be corrected. Her condition is so bad that she herself slept through that ordeal, and did not notice her husband's absence when she awoke.

His parents suffer in different ways, both fatal: "my father's body broke his spirit like a match," and "my mother's broken spirit took her body under the way a ship sinks after being disemboweled by an errant berg of ice" (135).

Two other relatives from Kohler's parents' generation figure prominently in the book. Kohler's Uncle Balt gets a section to himself, "Uncle Balt and the Nature of Being." He is introduced initially as the one who had been warning Kohler's mother about the storm, telling her to come downstairs, the day lightning shattered a window whose broken glass fell into her hair. Kohler describes him as "tall, thin, slightly cadaverous," with a weathered face and big knuckles. He farmed with a religious devotion, tending his land all by himself. What interests Kohler, though, about Uncle Balt is that he serves as "a metaphor for Being," because he was "a tall dark column of damp air, hole going nowhere—yes—wind across the mouth of a bottle" (121). Kohler compares Uncle Balt to a barnyard cat because he sees him so seldom, only at "dawn, dusk, and dinner," which made Uncle Balt "a man shaped of absence," who had "the intangible integrity of a hollow, a well's heavy wet deficiencies" (122). He died as he had lived his life, at work and in solitude, from a fall while trying to climb over a fence. His defining quality, presence-in-absence and absence-in-presence, prefigures Kohler's attempt to create a figure of Being with his tunnel. The description of Uncle Balt as "a tall dark column of damp air" makes him a vertical equivalent to the more or less horizontal long, dark column of air, the tunnel.

The other important figure from Kohler's parents' generation is his mother's sister, to whom he refers simply as "Auntie." Kohler's earliest memories of her are of visits in which she brings him candy, but later she and her mother (Kohler's "Gran") move in to the Kohlers' house, sharing a room. She works as a secretary at an office-supply firm, though eventually she gets fired. Kohler describes her as acting out of passive aggression: "her overbearing deference drove my dad crazy" (588); she "did things for people they didn't quite want done" (592); she was "the Princess of the Inappropriate Present" (597). She did in the Kohler home what she did at her jobs: starting with acts of efficiency and apparent generosity, she insinuated herself into everything. At the house, this process began with her taking over the laundry, mending, and ironing, and culminated in her taking "hold of the movement of life in our house" (597), even getting from Kohler's father's will at his death the use of the house for the rest of her life.

Like Uncle Balt, Auntie gives Kohler a metaphor for Being, in this case through a trunk she brings with her when she first arrives at the Kohlers' house. It is moved eventually to the attic, where one day young Billy Kohler steps inside it and lowers the lid, "to get the full feeling of that emptiness I'd entered" (591). The latch, though, catches ("I wasn't cabined, cribbed. I was coffined. I'd be buried in my box of being"), and Kohler panics: "If pure Being was pure panic, I knew what pure Being was." He finally hits the sides of the trunk hard enough to pop the latch and get out, but not before the experience imbues him with "a more manageable fright" (592) that seems to have stayed with him into adulthood. Auntie's trunk (with its intimation of "trunks") prefigures Kohler's wife's antique dressers (with their intimation of "drawers"); Gass uses both as metaphors for Being, with sexual overtones in each case, and both function as instruments of Kohler's humiliation and defeat.

10. Who are Kohler's family?

Kohler's wife, Martha, works as a curator for the local historical museum. She wants to open an antique store; toward that end, she collects antique dressers, which in the meantime clutter the attic and hallways in the Kohlers' house. She is not allowed to develop as a character, to have a voice or presence of her own other than as an object against whom Kohler can vent his spleen. Still, she is a "round character," in one sense of the term: Kohler repeatedly complains of her obesity, and throughout the book remains obsessed with her large breasts. He regularly grouses about their sleeping in separate beds and no longer having sex.

Their relationship was not always so arid, and Kohler still speaks fondly of their early tenderness, mentioning for example that in their sex play "we both called my cock **Herr Rickler** when it rose" (90). But he also makes clear how quickly their relationship cooled. In one of the book's twelve philippics, "The First Winter of My Married Life," Kohler describes the inhibiting effect of their living in a poorly constructed duplex. The other half of the duplex stood empty when the Kohlers rented theirs, so they did not anticipate any of the problems that arose as soon as the other side was occupied. Each half of the duplex mirrored the other, so the bedrooms and bathrooms abutted. That floor plan, combined with thin walls, meant that noises passed almost undiminished between the two halves of the house, making the Kohlers exaggeratedly self-conscious: "We were soon ashamed of our own sounds, as if every sign of life we made were a form of breaking wind" (335). They heard the other couple making love, so they became inhibited when making love themselves; they heard the other couple arguing, so they became aware of the frequency of their own arguments. "We heard ourselves," Kohler says, "as others might hear us," with results fatal to their relationship: "I ceased singing in the shower. We kissed only in distant corners, and as quietly as fish. We gave up our high-spirited games. Martha no longer cried out when she came, and I grew uncertain of her love" (336–37).

Martha and William have two young sons. The elder is named Carl, and the younger Adolf, though Kohler studiously avoids referring to him by name. The book offers no trustworthy explanation for

TWENTY QUESTIONS ON *THE TUNNEL*

why he is named Adolf, or why Kohler so dislikes him; it only cites the name as a source of dispute between the parents ("she hates the name," Kohler tells us, adding with his customary paranoia that she "chose it out of spite"), and tells us that Martha "gave the kid the name of my obsession" (371). Without any attempt at consistency with other explanations he gives for his marital problems, Kohler blames young Adolf for the animosity between himself and Martha, saying that after Adolf's birth "she cursed me with her coldness, and emptied me from her embrace like an armload of dirty clothes, a pot of chamber water."

Unlike Martha, the sons are mentioned infrequently, and seem seldom on Kohler's mind. He says, "My kids will not come to visit me. . . . I did not become my children. I spat them out like pits and they grew up as near and yet apart from me as weeds in a row of beans" (137–38). The same driving that represents his hatred of his father in "Learning to Drive" represents his hatred of his children in "Family Album," where he imagines that maybe "I'm going to back up over some tyke in my driveway" (370), and in the same paragraph he announces—as bluntly as his own father had declared that "he ain't mine"—that "I don't care" about them.

Kohler acts out his aggression against Martha by taking the dirt he is digging from under their basement, and emptying it into the drawers of her beloved antique dressers. The blue pun Kohler so enjoys about dirtying Martha's drawers finds its consummation in the incident in which he kills Martha's cat after it has scared him during his digging, which enables him to put her dead pussy in her drawers. Martha discovers the dirt, as Kohler must have known she eventually would, and near the end of the book she brings in a drawerful. She "rather rudely brushed by me and with a heartfelt hooof tipped the entire drawer over my manuscript," leaving it "beneath a heap of yellow, gray, and bluish dirt" (648–49). We are not told what other effects follow the crisis brought on by her discovering the dirt, because its first effect, apparently, is to enforce an end to Kohler's writing.

11. How do Kohler's lovers figure in the book?

Kohler identifies two lovers who have significant, lingering emotional significance for him. He has had relationships with others (a student he refers to as "Betty Boop," his affair with whom he is chastised for by his department chair, and a young woman named Ruth—nicknamed "Rue"—who gives him blow jobs but will not spread her legs), but to judge by the manner in which, and the relative infrequency with which, he mentions them, these affairs mattered less to him.

More than once Kohler rehearses the one romantic "shortened summer month together" that he spent with one of his lovers, Lou. He relishes the ease with which she inhabited her body, exclaiming hyperbolically that her soul was the same as her skin. He relishes her living so fully and consistently in the present, a denial of history he finds himself able to achieve only through her, but one that is represented by her insistence, over his protestations, on turning to the wall of their room a picture of a Civil War encampment. Kohler seldom uses religious language as praise, but does so about Lou, who as a sexual partner was able, he says, to take him to that condition in which, "in passing beyond pleasure, your defenses fall, your ego surrenders," and "you return, not to the clay you came from—the unfired vessel—but to the original moment of inspiration, when you were the unabbreviated breath of God" (560).

Kohler makes it clear that he loved Lou more than Lou loved him, apparently even from the beginning of their affair. He states the

TWENTY QUESTIONS ON *THE TUNNEL*

fact almost with fondness when he says she "would leave me with the same insouciance with which she joined me. . . . It was I who was supposed to be having an adventure, but it was she who had it" (556), but soon says it again with a more bitter tinge: "Notice," he says, "how 'lover' is mostly spelled by using 'over,' and 'sex' is two-thirds 'ex'" (560). He returns more than once to the rendezvous at a sidewalk café when she "gives him the sack," a figure of speech literalized on page 174 by reproducing the image of a grocery sack. He tells about their sexual game, "Do rivers," in which he would run his fingers across her back, each time naming the river whose path he pretends to trace. Even though one time near the end of the affair he feels compelled to write "YOU NO LONGER LOVE ME" in capital letters instead of "doing a river," he continues to treasure the memory of their affair so much that he says, "I would rather forget my children's names," a state of affairs he seems to want and almost achieves, than forget "the names of my rivers" (562).

Even though he does not "understand what makes another body so appealing" (107), Kohler does know that his love for Lou was strong because it stood in such stark opposition to the rest of his life. Everywhere else in his life, Kohler finds himself constantly and oppressively burdened by history. His relationship with his wife suffers from their personal history (their year in the thin-walled duplex, the birth of Adolf, and so on), and he perceives himself as identified closely with the Third Reich, living as a physical representative of that instance of man's inhumanity to man. After the fact, his aborted relationship with Lou adds to the burdensomeness of history, but for that one August, Lou intervenes and isolates the historian from history, liberating him—even in the guilty act of having an affair—from his oppressive guilt, so that for that moment, "the fingers which slipped through the enchanted forest of your twat" stop being the ones that threw "that rock on *Kristallnacht*" (110). "We were happy," he says, "because we had no history" (108). With *Guilt and Innocence* Kohler talked his way into history; with the scrawlings that become *The Tunnel* he tries to talk his way out.

Kohler's other significant lover, Susu, plays an opposite role. If Lou releases Kohler from history, Susu draws him down more deeply into it. Kohler portrays Susu as a femme fatale, a slender French woman singing in a seedy German bar, whose very song "was drawn to me as sucking insects are," and "was thirsty for my blood" (98). Susu becomes for Kohler a siren of psychic suicide, "the emptiness after the cliff's edge" (482). He meets her, "a silken sliver" reminiscent of the glass shards in his mother's hair, an "illicit wish" (103), in his student days, though later, while doing research for one of his books, he learns from "a stack of brutal documents" (99) that she had "roasted the thumbs of a dozen Jews" and eaten them while her German lover and his Nazi comrades watched (115). The thumbs become the point of connection between Susu's childishness and her brutality, two seemingly opposed characteristics that prove at root identical. "The name *Susu* stresses the syllabic replication that young children make in their prelanguage development ('mama,' 'dada,' and so forth)," reminding us that she "is fundamentally a child; she seems to have no will, no hardness of substance; she is small and frail; she is described as sucking a thumb. The familiar fact of childish thumbsucking, however, is drawn into a monstrous figural extension: the thumbs that Susu sucks are the thumbs of Jews killed by the Nazis."[51]

Though she had been "a commandant's whore," when the Nazis learned that she had gypsy blood they decapitated her. Less is told of the particulars of Kohler's relationship with Susu than of his relationship with Lou, but at the end of the book he claims a stronger identification with Susu. His attraction to Lou was attraction to his opposite, one who can shun history in favor of the present moment, but he loves Susu as his double: "it was Susu who was my soul's sort. She was success in the pure form of failure" (651). Lou saved him, if only briefly, but "Susu's where I burn" (491), no doubt because Susu remained a fantasy: their love remained imaginary, and therefore never eroded through the abrasive effects of reality, and never suffered a clear and definitive end, even when Susu was killed.

12. What is the significance of Kohler's colleagues?

Like the four friends in the biblical book of Job, Kohler's four departmental colleagues, each of whom he scorns, serve as foils for his own views of history and of life, though the reader must bear in mind that all descriptions are of the colleagues as seen through Kohler's thoroughly jaundiced eye. Each represents a possible view of history: "Planmantee the rationalist, Governali the romantic, Herschel the moderator, and Culp the joker and cynic. They are, of course, projections of [Kohler's] own conflicted sense of meaning: Is life explainable, tragic, bland, or just funny?"[52]

Of all his colleagues, none of whom he likes or respects, Kohler most vehemently hates Oscar Planmantee, a pompous pedantic who wears his Phi Beta Kappa key on a chain between the pockets of his vest and his Mensa insignia in a buttonhole. Planmantee—Kohler sometimes calls him "the Manatee"—was born in Fort Wayne, Indiana, and educated in Ohio, though he is ashamed of his origins, and tried to adopt a Viennese pose (having learned German during the war and married a Tyrolean woman, ten years his senior, who later left him).

If Kohler's love for Lou is linked to their unlikeness, his hatred of Planmantee is exacerbated by their similarity; Kohler, just like Planmantee, wishes desperately to be more German than he is. Kohler describes Planmantee as contentious, not confining "his objections merely to opinions," but "able to take exception to your posture, your point of view, your plan of study, your taste in sugary stewed tomatoes" (388–89). In regard to history, Planmantee is a positivist who considers nothing in the last hundred years worthy of historical study, and who tries to quantify everything: "the lines he drew and called History were every one of them medians, summaries, averages, on-the-wholes, inasmuch as human affairs fell, for him, under the same laws as rust, rot, mold, or mildew did" (394). Among his other reasons, Kohler hates Planmantee for reminding him of, and attempting to punish him for, his (apparently multiple) indiscretions with female students.

Kohler's next colleague, Tommaso Governali, a third-generation Italian American, has written a book called *Character Crucified on the Cross of the Historical Chronicle*. Kohler, who calls Governali's book "silly," describes him as "the nemesis of Planmantee," because he scorns Planmantee's positivism. Governali, an idealist, sees history on analogy with opera. "He doesn't entertain ideas," Kohler says, "he sings arias." If for Planmantee history resolves itself finally into statistics, for Governali history "is hysteria and histrionics. There is a pit, a proscenium, and a curtain—whatever the audience can see—but there is nothing going on behind the scenes: courtship and conspiracy take the form of duets" (400). In character, Governali "likes to insert himself in people's lives," whether by interrogating or empathizing. "He makes you suffer from his bartender's ear." After a time of successes generated by his book (public recognition, a Guggenheim grant, election to the Faculty Senate), Governali eventually

TWENTY QUESTIONS ON *THE TUNNEL*

suffers personal problems centered on his daughter, Lire, whose conception is rumored to have resulted from an affair between Governali's wife and a chemistry student. After Lire turns fifteen, she begins hanging around the campus, associating with hippy students, getting arrested at demonstrations, and so on. Eventually, Governali, trying to rein her in, pursues her to a local hangout, is given (without his knowledge) a drugged drink, enters "acid heaven," and is never the same, the promise of his early career never fulfilled.

Physically, Walter Henry Herschel, another of Kohler's colleagues, is short, stout, and gray-haired. In character, Herschel is a sympathetic listener, self-effacing, "the kind of failure no one notices, no one exults over, no one mourns, not only because Herschel never complains about anything, but because no one credits Herschel with ambition, purposes, urges, points of view, a tender ego, calculation" (414). Herschel holds the unenviable role of departmental pushover. He has "a wee M.A. from a wee-er school" (306), has not published a book, was tenured by "the pity of others," and is stuck perenially teaching only survey courses. His view of history is modest, moderate, and commonsensical: he believes in facts and truth, and the ability of an honest historian to identify the former and communicate the latter. Kohler has to work to repress his admiration of Herschel's willingness to entertain all sides of an issue, but he *does* repress it, viewing Herschel's open-mindedness as an intellectual flaw. "I call him the hedgehog because he is such a believer in both sides." Kohler says that "Herschel never declares, or asserts, or avers—I do that; Governali avows and Planmantee affirms; they do that—Herschel assents, or suggests; he elaborates, or gently opines" (182–83).

To his scorn Kohler adds some measure of sympathy for, or identification with, Governali and Herschel, but Charles Culp rivals Planmantee as an object of Kohler's unmitigated derision. "He is," Kohler says, "a punishment for my sins, a plague of boils.... After everyone else has walked out of my mind, he lingers like a bad smell" (156). Culp is writing "a limerickal history of the human race," in addition to a series of limericks (some quoted by Kohler in the book) each beginning with "I once went to bed with a nun." By using the limerick, which he describes as "false and lifeless" (177), Culp adopts a resolutely ironic stance toward history, reduces it to a language "designed to make everything appear to be stupid, callow, scarcely whelped" (166). Culp's irony and Kohler's cynicism reduce their relationship to "almost wholly one of tiresome repartee" (198).

Distancing himself from his colleagues' views of history, Kohler reserves for himself a view, more plausible to a "disappointed person," derived from that of his teacher, Magus Tabor.

13. What is the influence of "Mad Meg"?

Kohler's most significant professional and intellectual influence was Magus Tabor, usually referred to as "Mad Meg," the teacher under whom Kohler studied in Germany in the 1930s. The influence is strong enough that it seems almost as if Kohler were "channeling" Tabor, or trying to, leading Arthur M. Saltzman to see "the subtle bond between master and pupil in *The Tunnel*" as a reiteration of the spiritual bond in *Omensetter* that he calls "the *haunting* of Reverend Jethro Furber by the ghost of Reverend Pike."[53] So significant is Tabor's influence that Kohler's first rumination, "Life in a Chair," talks about spending his writing career in "the great Tabor's own chair, which I had shipped from Germany" (6). Tabor, a specialist in Greek and Roman history, contended that historians do not merely

TWENTY QUESTIONS ON *THE TUNNEL*

recount history, but rather create it. "Tabor believed that anything of which you could form a passionate conception automatically *was,* because the pure purpose of things lay in their most powerful description" (248). History is subject to the most potent verbal account, making Tabor's theory a narrower version, with language standing for the whole mind, of Wallace Stevens's more general view that "The world is at the mercy of the strongest mind in it, whether that strength is the strength of sanity or insanity, cunning or good-will."[54] Historical truth, in Tabor's formulation, is made not by those who do the most important things, but by those who tell the best stories about what has been done, itself a view that mimics Stevens's claim that "the final belief is to believe in a fiction, which you know to be a fiction."[55] Thus, for example, according to Tabor and Kohler, "when a man writes the history of your country in another language, he is bent on conquest," which occurs not by getting a white flag raised or a surrender signed, but by replacing "your past, and all your methods of communication, your habits of thinking, feeling, and perceiving, your very way of being, with his own" (271).

Tabor's view about history corresponds to his own personality: "he was an absolute actor," like Shakespeare's evil Richard III claims to be when he says "I can add colors to the chameleon, / Change shapes with Proteus for advantages, / And set the murderous Machiavel to school."[56] Tabor is, therefore, "perfectly capable of raising and sustaining a purely rhetorical erection" (250). So it is against Tabor *and* his view of history that Kohler has to struggle, to keep Tabor's habits of thinking and ways of being from overwhelming his own, but he seems not to succeed, instead allowing Tabor to become in his mind "the spiritual founder of the Party of the Disappointed People" (266).

In addition to his sharing shiftiness with Richard III, Tabor shares misanthropy with another of Shakespeare's characters, Coriolanus. Mad Meg rails against the "crowds—these masses in the plaza," calling them "those sweaty heads below the scented hands and front porch of the pope," and saying "the only expectations all these creatures have in common's common death," these "whiny widdlepissers" who would have "barbecued Christ's bones if they had twigged to the thought of it and had the sauce—these—**these** anchovies, these sauerkrauts, these little lilliputzers" (127). His scorn echoes that of Coriolanus, who (after they turn on him for not flattering them) calls the crowd "You common cry of curs, whose breath I hate / As reek o' th' rotten fens, whose loves I prize / As the dead carcasses of unburied men / That do corrupt my air."[57] Kohler, of course, adopts Mad Meg's misanthropy as his own.

Tabor's free identification with others, as if he had multiple personalities, extends beyond Shakespearean characters. Robert Kelly points out that Tabor's hypocoristic, "Mad Meg," comes from "Brueghel's painting of the madwoman," and then connects the painting to yet another identification, this one within *The Tunnel* itself: "Kohler's mother," Kelly observes, "is Margaret too, also a Meg, so the novel has two Mad Megs," since "Kohler winds up his youth by putting her into a madhouse."[57] As previous chapters have pointed out, Gass often declares in essays and interviews how important names are to his fiction; in this case the name "Mad Meg" establishes Tabor's role as a surrogate parent for Kohler.

If Tabor's nickname connects him to the confessional project Kohler is actually writing, his given name connects him to the scholarly project Kohler is supposed to be writing, the preface to *Guilt and Innocence,* by embodying "precisely the metaphor of history as Gass presents it in this work. A magus was a priest-wiseman of ancient Persia, adept in the occult sciences of astrology and alchemy, who, as a consequence of his superior knowledge and abilities to do mysterious and wonderful things, was held in awe and feared by the common people," just as Tabor's students, including Kohler, hold him in awe, since his "words thunder and pound like a drumbeat (a 'tabor' is, after all, a drum)."[59] The name also relates Kohler to his teacher, because Kohler's status as a "disappointed person" derives in part from his inability to fulfill his wish to be, and be treated as, a magus, and because Kohler's relentless writing develops, as it drags out through 652 pages, the character of a drumbeat.

14. What is the point of the PdP?

Even before the written text of the novel begins, the book presents drawings of "The Pennants of Passive Attitudes and Emotions," the "PdP banner," the "Medal for ingratitude," and an unidentified insignia, complementing them later (on pages 266 and 288) with other images of PdP paraphernalia.

The PdP, the Party of the Disappointed People, an imaginary political organization Kohler has created to fulfill the function of all political parties, "to organize and institutionalize human weakness" (533), consists of an underclass defined so that it includes, Kohler believes, everyone. "Our" disappointment stems not from simple mutability, though Kohler does think that "if things did not pass away, our interest in them would" (286). Nor does human disappointment derive from simple ill fortune. Born into consistent ill fortune, "we would finally accommodate our needs to necessity; we'd acclimate ourselves." Even the contrast between good fortune and ill fortune does not generate the disappointment of Kohler's PdP. Echoing Thomas Hardy's sonnet "Hap," where the speaker says it would be easier to endure suffering if "some vengeful god" (rather than "Crass Casualty") were causing it, Kohler says, "that contrast" between good fortune and ill fortune, "if it were carved in stone, if it were God's inflexible rule, could be endured, and poets would find ways to praise it" (286).

The disappointment results from our belief "that life might have been otherwise; that it's been wrongly lived, and hence lost" (286); it comes from "not having held what was in our hands to hold; not having felt the feelings we were promised by our parents, friends, and lovers; not having got the simple goods we were assured we had honestly earned and rightfully had coming" (366). Kohler feels this disappointment in himself, and attributes it to the Nazis; it is the disappointment that becomes hatred, and makes people unpredictable and misanthropic and malevolent. "What do we protest? That we die alive. Who shall blame us when we turn on our murderers then, and murder them?" (287). This disappointment becomes what Kohler calls "the fascism of the heart."

The fascism of the heart, as the point of connection between Kohler's historical interest in the Nazis and his preoccupation with his own life, "is the subject of this book. The Third Reich is seen as the *active* uprising of the *passive* attitudes and emotions."[60] Kohler identifies its source when he says, "Loss in life: that's what I mourn for; that's what we all mourn for, all of us who have been touched by the fascism of the heart." Kohler is the biblical Job with an irrational and inflated sense of entitlement. Job complains because he has upheld his side of the (perceived) contract; he has been "blameless and upright," and has "feared God and turned away from evil." He complains when he gets nothing good in return for his own good actions. Kohler complains, too, but he thinks the bargain is one-sided. The world owes him more than it has given him, not as the rightful response to good actions he has done, but "just because."

Merle Rubin asks, "Why should Kohler—who has a home, a family, a job with tenure—feel such disappointment?" He answers that, according to the novel, "disappointment is a phenomenon more pervasive than hunger, poverty, or homelessness, affecting all levels of society."[61] But there is one more step to be taken in his chain of reasoning: that disappointment of the type Kohler harbors is pervasive because what one expects from the world always starts out as distinct from what one owes to the world. One begins life expecting to receive what one needs/wants from the world, but only later (if at all) does one learn a sense of obligation toward the world. The two may become linked as a means of curbing (or denying) disappointment, after which only the complaints of the few "blameless and upright" people like Job are accorded legitimacy, but *everyone* has a complaint.

Kohler's claim that his complaint is like everyone else's does not entail that his feelings about it are of normal or average intensity; in fact, he says they are not. "The malice I bear has borne me to my knees. I have resentment to spare for a flood; my loose change would millionaire most men" (43). The intensity of his resentment is important to Kohler. "Hate has given force and purpose to my life. I've studied it. It's studied me." Kohler has no sense of obligation toward the world, and he therefore refuses to accept any distinction between legitimate and illegitimate forms of disappointment.

Even if the resentment is universal, and even if it were more often as intense as Kohler's, that still would not by itself make Kohler's case that the disappointment disappointed people feel makes them (or, as Kohler sees things, us) potentially as murderous as the Nazis. The missing premise is supplied by David Hume, with whose *Treatise of Human Nature* at least the philosopher Gass, if not the historian Kohler, would be on familiar terms. If humans were "rational animals," as Aristotle claims, we would be at least potentially able to overcome our resentment. But Hume and Kohler think we are not rational animals. "Nothing is more usual in philosophy," Hume says, "than to talk of the combat of passion and reason," and "to give the preference to reason." But Hume argues that "reason alone can never be a motive to any action of the will," and reason "can never oppose passion in the direction of the will."[62] Applying this to the PdP, they (we) are dangerous and unpredictable because the passions, not the reason, prompt us to action. Even highly educated and unusually reflective people like Kohler himself are not reasonable. We act out of what we feel, says Kohler, not what we think, and we feel resentment, so the motives of his own puny and isolated actions, with their relatively minor effects on others, are identical with the motives of the Nazi's monumental and well-coordinated actions, with their immeasurable impact on others.

15. Why the references to Kristallnacht?

For at least one night, Kohler participated in the actions of the Nazis; he reports having been complicit in what came to be called Kristallnacht. As hostility toward Jews increased in Germany during the time leading up to World War II, Jews were required to visibly identify their shops as Jewish-owned. On the night of November 9, 1938, rioting Germans vandalized and looted many of those shops. Kohler,

TWENTY QUESTIONS ON *THE TUNNEL*

awakened at about three a.m. by noises in the streets, got out of bed, dressed, and went into the street. Immediately he was taken for a Jew and threatened, but he escaped. He reports having "wandered about. The streets were empty except for occasional gangs. The windows of the Jewish shops were being smashed" (329). He saw convoys of trucks, a synagogue being burned, small groups of men. Eventually he ran into three of his friends from the university, who reported having seen much more vandalism than Kohler himself had seen. The four joined others drifting in a group toward the sound of breaking glass. Eventually, Kohler threw a paving stone through the window of a Jewish grocer's shop. The breaking of the window, though, proved anticlimactic: "There was more pitter than patter, I think. Now, if I wished, I could steal perhaps a cabbage or a big beet" (331). He retrieved the stone and broke another window, this time not belonging to a Jew.

Kohler's attitude toward his remembered behavior that night more closely resembles embarrassment than guilt or remorse. As if he affirmed Antonio Porchia's hypothesis that "evil is everything, and that good is only a beautiful desire for evil,"[63] Kohler seems not to feel sorry that his actions that night were bad, but instead to feel merely humiliated that they were ugly. He does not take the window-breaking in the way that his reader surely will, as a reminder that "Evil is terrible and also very close."[64]

His participation in Kristallnacht creates the most specific point of contact between the two histories on the correlation of which the book is built, his personal history and the history of Nazi Germany, and suggests that "Kohler's personal history contains the seeds of the Holocaust; Kohler, in his very being, is a fascist." His throwing the rock "returns to pollute his thoughts and his dreams, and is in large part the principal event of his history, both in the book (public) and in his preface (private)." Still, the only violation he acknowledges, the only one that "he himself feels deeply," is of the windows, not the shopowners, because of "his reverence for windows as a meeting ground of the mind and whatever is meant by reality beyond the glass."[65]

16. Why are there so many windows in the book?

The window, which represents the ambiguity of our connection to the world, our looking out on a world from which the very looking out separates us, has appeared as a metaphor regularly in Gass's previous fiction. For example, in "Icicles" the narrator uses the window to represent the fearfulness of the protagonist, Fender. Though the windows allow Fender to observe the icicles that are the object of his fascination, they also allow others to see him, awareness of which makes him afraid even to touch his tongue to the window to cool it after a hot bite of pot pie. In "Icicles," the narrator leaves the reader to infer the importance of windows to Fender, but in *The Tunnel,* the first-person narrator meditates on windows explicitly, devoting one of the book's twelve major sections to discussing "why windows are important to me."

Windows matter, Kohler says, because "it's always a window which lets me see" (282). The windows in his home office (overlooking the garden) and his office at the university (overlooking the public park) "are the porches of appearance. Through them move the only uncoded messages which I receive" (282–83). They let him look out, in other words, on an ahistorical world, a world not subject to Tabor's oppressive view of history-as-a-coded-message-and-*only*-a-coded-message. They open onto a nostalgic, precynical world into which he occasionally permits himself a glimpse, as when he pines

TWENTY QUESTIONS ON *THE TUNNEL*

for his one-time lover, Lou. They give him a way of looking out on others while remaining concealed himself. Windows give Kohler a way to manipulate concealment and exposure, as do his two other self-confessed significant spaces, "the white of the page, and the black of the board" (311).

Windows also figure in several of the crucial events narrated in *The Tunnel:* during his stay in Germany during the 1930s, Kohler spent, he tells us, a great deal of time secretly watching the apartment opposite his, peering for that purpose through two windows, his own and the opposed apartment's; it is a window that a storm shatters in Kohler's youth, sending down a glitter of glass on his mother's hair; Kohler claims to have thrown a brick through a window on Kristallnacht; and so on.

Even moving windows figure importantly in Kohler's life. His recollection of the car wreck from his childhood begins with him at a window, "watching the roadside go by as dreamily as it was watching me" until "I heard from my father half an inarticulate outcry and my head was slammed into the watching window" (232). He hears "a series of terrible sounds: of rending metals, shattering glass, pissing vapors, unstaged screams," but when he sees the wreck, he sees through the mediation of the window his head had just hit. "Through that window, back on the highway we had so abruptly fled, I saw two automobiles still shuddering from the force of their collision." One indicator of the severity of the wreck is that "glass began to patter upon the roof of our Chevrolet where we were stopped upon the shoulder." The event made nature itself assume in his mind the fragility of glass. "The dust still rose in rivulets, making the air seem to shake as if it were a pane of glass in the process, like the sky, of coming to pieces" (233).

Through these various functions of windows, one metafictional constant runs: the window always advances a metaphorical ideal for lucidity in writing. "I'd like," Kohler says, "to look below my eyes and see not language staring back at me, not sentences or single words or awkward pen lines, but a surface clear and burnished as a glass" (48–49). Gass wants this novel to be like a tunnel, certainly, but also like a window: framing and exposing a perceptual/conceptual field, and protecting the reader from that field, positioning the reader as an observer.

17. What concept of history operates in the book?

Kohler's theory of history is nothing new; Shelley wrote two centuries ago that "all the great historians, Herodotus, Plutarch, Livy, were poets,"[66] and more recently a philosopher/novelist about whom Gass has written, Elias Canetti, said succinctly that "what a poet doesn't see never happened."[67] Kohler's view of history closely matches the one Gass himself professes in his essays, itself a version of Emerson's, and ultimately Aristotle's, valorizing poetry over history.

Emerson says events and facts metamorphose over time into poetic meanings: they become fictional. "Time dissipates to shining ether the solid angularity of facts." Nothing can make a fact *stay* a fact. "Babylon, Troy, Tyre, Palestine, and even early Rome are passing already into fiction. The Garden of Eden, the sun standing still in Gibeon, is poetry thenceforward to all nations. Who cares what the fact was, when we have made a constellation of it to hang in heaven an immortal sign?"[68] His view furthers a line of thought begun by Aristotle, who distinguished historian from poet by saying that "the one describes the thing that has been, and the other a kind of thing

TWENTY QUESTIONS ON *THE TUNNEL*

that may be," making poetry the more important because its statements are "universals, whereas those of history are singulars."[69] According to Aristotle, what matters is the universal, which is the province of poetry. Emerson pushes Aristotle's position: instead of saying that history is always singular and never matters while poetry is always universal and always matters, Emerson says that whenever history does matter, it matters because it has been changed from singularity to universality, which happens only on condition that it become poetry.

In the spirit of Aristotle and Emerson, Gass writes that "the real power of historical events lies in their descriptions; only by virtue of their passage into language can they continue to occur, and once recorded (even if no more than as gossip), they become peculiarly atemporal, residing in that shelved-up present which passes for time in a library" (*FFL,* 126). Such a view opposes, for instance, the view of history espoused by Abraham Lincoln in the Gettysburg Address when he stated that "the world will little note nor long remember what we say here, but it can never forget what [the Union soldiers] did here." Lincoln holds that "actions speak louder than words," and the consequences of the soldier's deeds will be independent of any later words. Gass's view implies instead that the most important "deed" at Gettysburg was Lincoln's speech, and that the Battle of Gettysburg became the most famous of the war not because of its importance per se to victory or defeat but because Lincoln's words were spoken about it and shared its name. "What we remember of our own past," Gass says, "depends very largely on what of it we've put our tongue to telling and retelling. It's our words, roughly, we remember; oblivion claims the rest—forgetfulness. Historians make more history than the men they write about" (*FFL,* 126–27).

That view becomes amenable to Gass and functional in this book because it facilitates Gass's correlation between the history of nations and personal history, between fascism and "fascism of the heart," by drawing the same conclusion Emerson does, that "we are always coming up with the emphatic facts of history in our private experience and verifying them here. All history becomes subjective; in other words there is properly no history, only biography."[70] Seen from a different angle, Mad Meg's insistence that "there is no such thing as *Wahrheit* (truth)" but "only competing texts of *Dichtung* (poetic, fictional composition)" correlates precisely to "Gass's definition of fascism: making a work of art out of real life—making things fit in to suit none but the needs of the artifact under construction."[71]

One might trace the view of history in *The Tunnel* even farther back, beyond Aristotle to the Platonic valorizing of soul over body. Its roots lie in the assumption that what matters most is mental rather than physical. So Gass says in an essay, "On the whole (the ruins of cities are an exception, as are the records of rocks and bones), the principal consequences of any event lie not in its immediate physical effects, but in the amount of paper it generates, the degree of human attention which it stimulates."[72] Some events *ought* to generate more paper than they do, though. "I have always felt that historians spent far too much time on wars and revolutions, the rise and fall of kingdoms," which "say or change remarkably little about us in the long run." They ought to attend more carefully to "whatever alters the nature of the human mind, such as the creation of abstract ideas, the discovery of logic," and so on. This line of thought brings Gass around to the key premise on which the view of history in *The Tunnel* stands: "These events and others like them belong in the center of the stage, *since it is human consciousness that counts*."[73] Given that premise, it should surprise no reader that Kohler moves so readily from the "wars and revolutions, the rise and fall of kingdoms" that Hitler helped cause to a form of human consciousness, personal disappointment, that he thinks made Hitler possible.

Nor should it surprise any reader that Kohler accepts his knowledge of history as reason to adopt a pessimistic stance toward the future. When Gass argues in an essay against assuming that better art will survive and worse will not, he reminds his reader that history itself displays no consciousness. "We should not blame 'history'" for the fact that the good guys don't always win. "History is not an agent who goes about trampling traditions into dust, ending lives, stifling others, despoiling the land and poisoning the sea." The major difference between Emerson's view of history and the view Gass and Kohler share is that Emerson postulates a benevolent, transcendent consciousness guiding history. Gass and Kohler, after dismissing such a transcendent consciousness, are left with history as merely "humanity on its rampage. Considering the frequency of natural calamities, our treatment of warfare as a seasonal sport, and the insatiable squirrelyness of human greed, it should be an occasion for surprise that anything excellent survives."[74]

A more popular view, that knowledge of history is ennobling and "the value of history" results from its presenting us "with something which is at the same time real and better than ourselves, something which can draw us upward,"[75] would lead to a narrator very different from Kohler, but the view of history Gass holds is consistent with the consciousness—Kohler's—he creates.

18. What concept of autobiography operates in the book?

As part of his tale of "the Sunday drive," Kohler recalls his family stopping by the side of the road at harvest time and gathering ripe food from others' crops. "Uninvited strays, we rooted even in the treetops. Not as useful as the wolves who weeded out the weak, we grabbed hard corn to grate into cakes, sidling down the stiffly military rows, cutting ourselves on the coarse leaves, stealing to keep our weaknesses alive. At least, as a kid, I felt that way about it" (224). He contrasts "this pilfering" with "the stealing of apples from neighborhood trees, or grapes from nearby arbors, a bunch of rhubarb or a hard brown pear," because small boys would be expected to commit the latter, but the former was "organized, approved, overseen, and executed by adults, those sources of righteousness, wisdom, and rule" (224).

Kohler's concluding the list with a pear cues the reader to recognize this recollection as a mirror-image of Augustine's recollection in the *Confessions* of stealing pears as a boy. In Augustine's case, he commits his crime with "some other wretched youths," and tells the story to show his innate depravity (that his pleasure lay "in the sin itself and not in those pears") and his redemption by God from depravity.[76] Kohler makes a point of how his pear-stealing differed because he, the boy, "would grow hot with fear and shame," but was encouraged to steal by the adults; so *The Tunnel* depicts a world without redemption, in which people mature into ever worse beings. Kohler, like Augustine, is confessing, but without the sense that the process will save him.

Augustine worries from the beginning of his confessions what form will make them efficacious. Kohler is explicit about the problem less often, but shares the worry. "When I write about the Third Reich, or now, when I write about myself, is it truly the truth I want? What *do* I want? to find out who I am? What is the good of that? I want to feel a little less uneasy." (Like Augustine, who famously wanted rest.) "We drag our acts behind us like a string of monsters. I am the Reich,

TWENTY QUESTIONS ON *THE TUNNEL*

the third son, the remains. This sort of thing—confession—this father-forgive-me stuff—is not in my line. My thoughts fly out like Zeno's arrow, still to stand. No, nor's the tone. My customary tone is scholarly. I always move with care," (also like Augustine) "and I've been praised for weight, the substance of my thought. But it's not the way I feel I want to speak now, and I realize (I've come to it as I write) that my subject's far too serious for scholarship, for history, and I must find another form before I let what's captive in me out" (106–7).

The Tunnel's connection with the *Confessions* receives confirmation in other ways, as when Kohler spends a paragraph on pages 514–15 debating with himself the relative merits of Manicheanism, the religion Augustine professed before his conversion to Christianity, denial of which provides one of the *Confessions*' primary themes, but a religion that would be obscure had not Augustine's rejection of it made it famous. In addition, Kohler reiterates the connection to Augustine explicitly: "I am digging a well—a deep one—for sieges—with walls like Byzantine mosaics: ah, how the colors would glow, the forms amaze, could we but see them! Will there be animals on them, as at Altamira? No. There will be thoughts, set down in the shapes of animals sometimes, as in St. Augustine" (553).

So clearly citing Augustine, whose *Confessions* helped create the genre of autobiography, calls attention to autobiography as an issue in *The Tunnel,* but the reversals indicate that the posture toward autobiography will be one of questioning rather than acceptance. For one thing, the difference between the writer and the narrator already raises questions, as in question 8 ("Is Kohler really William Gass?") above. Kohler claims *The Tunnel* is autobiographical: Gass claims that it is not. Can one speak meaningfully of an autobiography of a fictional character? Is an autobiography ever of anyone but a fictional character? If Gass claimed it as his own autobiography, would it be any less or more fictional? After all, Gass *claims* to have deliberately made it seem more like his own autobiography than it actually is: "The resemblances between myself and the narrator are wholly trivial, I think, but I did emphasize them in order to test the reader's sophistication (a test many reviewers failed). Though the common reader takes shelter in autobiography as if from rain, the identification they should make, and what the book suggests, is with the narrator and his narrowness and spite."[77] By maintaining this distinction between writer and narrator, *The Tunnel* tries to take advantage of the possibilities of autobiography, without allowing its readers "shelter."

The withholding of shelter results from Kohler's upping the confessional ante. Gass complains about autobiographers' tendency "to do partials, to skip the dull parts and circle the pits of embarrassment. Autobiographers flush before examining their stools. Are there any motives for the enterprise that aren't tainted with conceit or a desire for revenge or a wish for justification?" (*FAF,* 181). The only way to avoid such "partials," such conceit, would be to portray oneself as a wholly despicable person. Even that would be partial, but in a way less directly susceptible to vanity, less likely to be guilty of the vice implied by Leopardi's observation "It seems rare in our age to find a widely praised person whose own mouth is not the source of that praise."[78] Besides, in Gass's view at least, if not Kohler's, "to have written an autobiography is already to have made yourself a monster. Some, like Rousseau and Saint Augustine, capitalize on this fact and endeavor to hide deceit behind confession. Of course, as Freud has told us, they always confess to what their soul is convinced is the lesser crime" (*FAF*, 181).

Autobiography is the natural genre for Kohler because it is a diminishment—a "corruption"—of history, just the form one would predict for a disgruntled historian narrator in a novel by the writer who penned this indictment of the practice of history:

> Once upon a time history concerned itself only with what it considered important, along with the agents of these actions, the contrivers of significant events, and the forces that such happenings enlisted or expressed. . . . However, as machines began to replicate objects, and little people began to multiply faster than wars or famines could reduce their numbers, and democracy arrived to flatter the multitude and tell them they ruled, and commerce flourished, sales grew, and money became the really risen god, then numbers replaced significant individuals, the trivial assumed the throne (which was a camp chair on a movie set), and history looked about for gossip, not for laws, preferring lies about secret lives to the intentions of Fate. (*FAF,* 184–85)

Those "lies about secret lives" are lies not only because of what they *do* tell, but also because of what they strategically do not tell. "What gets left out? that I read the papers. What gets left out? that I ate potatoes. What gets left out? that I saved my snot for several years. . . . What gets left out? what demeans me; what does not distinguish me from anyone else: bowel movements, movie favorites, bottles of scotch" (*FAF,* 189). That material, typically left out of accounts of lives, is what we get 652 pages of in *The Tunnel.*

19. What is the meaning of the book's central events?

In an unpublished synopsis of *The Tunnel,* speaking about the action of the book, Gass himself admits that "there is scarcely any at all. The main action, aside from writing these pages, is the presumed, possible, digging of a tunnel by the narrator out of the basement of his own house. Since he could simply walk out of his front door, the pointlessness of this activity has to be stressed. The trapped character does everything symbolically, nothing actually." That account slightly exaggerates the situation, since (as mentioned in question 4 ("What are some of the book's predecessors?") above) several events get recounted in *The Tunnel:* the blown-out window, the car wreck, and so on. It would not be an exaggeration, though, to point out how distorted the relative weight given to events seems when Kohler depicts them. The distortion occurs in at least two ways: first, through the presumed correspondence between large-scale public, political events and small-scale private ones, and second, through the unusual attention devoted to events normally considered unimportant.

James Wolcott identifies the first distortion when he observes that "the big theatrical revelation in *The Tunnel*" occurs late in the book, in "a recounting of the disastrous birthday party for young Willie. The German catastrophe Kohler contemplates is an elaborate, sloppy fake-front. It isn't the Holocaust that's haunting Gass, it's alcoholism: a drunken mother dashing the hopes she's raised."[79] Once Kohler posits a uniformity of motivation among people, once he assumes that we are *all* "disappointed people," then he can explain any disappointment in terms of any other, and the Holocaust—the murder of millions—can serve as the "fake-front" for his petty private sufferings. In that way, the birthday party really *is* the most important event in the novel. Kohler has devoted his career to writing about the Holocaust because no one will give him a job for writing about what really matters to him, namely that his drunken mother couldn't even manage to throw him a birthday party when he was a child.

TWENTY QUESTIONS ON *THE TUNNEL*

The first distortion, the correspondence between personal drama, family drama, and sociopolitical drama, reveals Kohler's loss of perspective, his inability to assess the relative importance of events. That loss of perspective leads him to spend what seems like an inordinate amount of time on a lot of seemingly trivial matters. Nowhere is this attention to triviality more apparent in the book than in the section called "Around the House" (pp. 437 ff.). Beginning with a description of the sound of his alarm clock's ticking, Kohler moves to other banal events and items, including devoting more than a full page to the process of relieving himself. He notes that "unfortunately, I fart a lot," and painstakingly observes than when he wipes himself after defecating, "I usually pull off three sheets and fold them over to make one thick square" (438), continuing in grotesque detail: "I just make a pass and drop the result in the john as if I'd picked up a bug in a glove of Kleenex. Then I sit there a minute and think about it. . . . Three more sections are folded as before; my euphemistic visit is executed with the same motion, but now I push harder, and manage a more vigorous swipe. . . . With the third three I rub back and forth, as if I were polishing a car, and sometimes pinch the paper over for a fresh edge" (439). He tells us that he does not "study the condition of [his] stools" afterward, and reveals the technique he uses on the toilet lever.

So much seemingly gratuitous detail may diminish the level of drama in the book, making it subject to Wallace Stevens's critique of imagism in poetry: "Not all objects are equal. The vice of imagism was that it did not recognize this."[80] Nevertheless, the prominence of such quotidiana fulfills a principle Gass has defended elsewhere by asserting that "what we tend to lose with such a stress on traumas," devoting attention in fiction almost exclusively to "important" events, "is any feel for the weight of the ordinary, any sense of the accretions or the erosions of every day, the impact on the camel of each added straw, or the strength of the back each threatens to break" (*FFL,* 170). Kohler asserts that those mundane, "unimportant" straws, those disappointments, *do* add up, and become in the end backbreaking.

Gass has also asserted that the mundane and seemingly gratuitous matters on which Kohler lavishes such attention are also the ones that most accurately reveal our natures. Showing characters involved in "great" events may make for dramatic literature, but "in our world it's very hard for us to lead a tragic life, say, because it's frittered away in pratfalls."[81] Gass prepares us for Kohler by having the narrator of "In the Heart of the Heart of the Country" declare that, if human nature is to be depicted synecdochally (presenting a part to represent the whole), defecation does so more accurately than making love or declaring war. "It's not surprising that the novelists of the slums, the cities, and the crowds, should find that sex is but a scratch to ease a tickle, that we're most human when we're sitting on the john, and that the justest image of our life is in full passage through the plumbing" (*HHC,* 194).

20. Is *The Tunnel* a "great book"?

This chapter began by noting Gass's stated ambition for *The Tunnel,* that it be a "great book," and now, circling back to question 1, which asked about other readers' assessments, invites the reader, having considered *The Tunnel* at some length, to locate his or her own judgment between Steven Moore's effusive proclamation that "*The Tunnel* is a stupendous achievement and obviously one of the greatest novels of the century, a novel to set beside the masterpieces of Proust, Joyce,

TWENTY QUESTIONS ON *THE TUNNEL*

and Musil"[82] and James Bowman's less generous position, that "it will be years before anyone who values his position in the literary world will be able to say out loud what anyone with any sense makes of it now: it's a load of crap."[83]

To the dismissal, Gass himself provides the soundest rebuttal. The book would be "a load of crap" if its narrator were "a man so monstrous as to bear no resemblance to anyone [we] know, only to Nazis, and other ancient historical figures."[84] But, quoting Sinclair Lewis's insistence that no country in the world can be more hysterical than America, Gass contends that "Hitler's bunch" was worse than us only "because they had the opportunity. And opportunity is what another year like 1935 might provide" (171). It is true that Kohler "is sorrowful, without hope," and no longer expects the uprising he wishes for, but also true that "he is there, waiting, nevertheless, just underground, rather quiet, like the web worm in the sod, on the off chance, just in case." *The Tunnel* asks "How German are we?", a question Gass considers important because "its marvelous music, its profound philosophy, its adept science, its great literature, its industry and discipline" raised German culture "higher than the Alps," but could not "prevent the world's worst moral catastrophe." The failure of German culture therefore "casts doubt on the character of our every success, and makes suspicious even our simplest, plainest, most innocent-seeming acts." *The Tunnel*'s answer to the question "How German are we?" is "very."

In thus confronting his readers with a dark but plausible vision of humanity, derived from what is widely considered the most tragic historical event of the last century, Gass ensures that his novel cannot be merely "a load of crap." That, however, does not ensure that it will rival the works of Proust, Joyce, Musil, or the other authors

Gass cites as sharing his pessimistic view of humanity: Swift, Dostoevsky, Céline, and Sinclair Lewis. Indeed, Gass seems not to have enjoyed unmitigated success at either of the aims he himself identifies for *The Tunnel,* first, "the construction of a complex consciousness which is meant to be unique to Kohler, yet whose inner character is supposed to stand for the intellectual, on the one hand, and everyman, on the other," and second, "the construction of the ultimate anti-novel, which denies and defies all the ordinary methods of narration, plot, character, and so on. It is the opposite of history."[85]

Gass fails to achieve the first because a book is not a consciousness (despite Gass's protestations on this point), so whatever he manages by inventing Kohler, Gass does not "construct a consciousness." Nor is Kohler's character unqualified in its representation of "the intellectual" and "everyman." Kohler represents well the resentment that is at least latent in all humans, and also its potential destructiveness, but his resentment certainly boils much nearer the surface and proves easier to incite than in most persons, whether intellectuals or not. As for the second aim, Gass does choose to deemphasize plot and to use a self-absorbed first-person narrator, but a few typographical tricks and pictures of pennants hardly makes *The Tunnel* an anti-novel, much less the *ultimate* anti-novel. The techniques Gass uses in *The Tunnel* may have seemed out of the ordinary at the time he conceived the novel more than thirty years ago, but no longer seemed extraordinary by the time of its publication. That even a writer like Eudora Welty, who relies on "ordinary methods" of narration, plot, and character, still construes novels as *an* (if not *the*) opposite of history, following not chronology but "the continuous thread of revelation,"[86] makes it difficult to construe *The Tunnel* as an anti-novel at all.

TWENTY QUESTIONS ON *THE TUNNEL*

Toward an assessment of *The Tunnel,* one useful tool comes, appropriately enough, from a Jewish scholar in a book about the Hebrew Bible. Meir Sternberg distinguishes between underreading (not reading enough into a text), overreading (reading too much into a text), misreading (reading in bad faith, so as to find something in the text whether it is there or not), and counterreading (seeing in a text something irreconcilable with a sound interpretation). Sternberg makes the distinction in order to argue that the Bible is "virtually impossible to counterread," not least because the Bible's "narrator is absolutely and straightforwardly reliable."[87] Because of its resistance to counterreading, the Bible's truth value depends very little on the reader: "follow the biblical narrator ever so uncritically, and by no great exertion you will be making tolerable sense of the world you are in, the action that unfolds, the protagonists on stage, and the point of it all" (51).

In contrast, *The Tunnel* has an absolutely *un*reliable narrator, is *very* susceptible to counterreading, and demands significant exertion to determine "the point of it all." Its susceptibility to counterreading means that the value of *The Tunnel* will depend, even more than that of most books, on the reader. *The Tunnel* is a Socratic dialogue, but the *reader* has to be simultaneously Socrates enough to question Kohler, and Crito enough to accept the questioning of his or her own motives and intentions. Unlike the Bible (on Sternberg's account), which, thanks to its reliable narrator, holds value for any reader regardless of her or his level of competence, the value of *The Tunnel,* with its unreliable, despicable narrator serving as a "devil's advocate," will depend on the reader's ability—and will—to elicit vantages Kohler does not state. The haunting paradox is that, if Kohler is right about humanity, there will be no readers thus equipped.

CHAPTER SEVEN

Four Movements: *Cartesian Sonata*

Steven Moore compares *Cartesian Sonata* to *Willie Masters' Lonesome Wife,* on the premise that both books "concern what might be called aesthetic vision: the ability to see similarities and thus make metaphors, the enhanced attention to objects and their aesthetic properties and possibilities, a concern with forms and patterns (both real and imagined), and an obsession with the representational value of words."[1] *Cartesian Sonata* seems calculated to elicit such a comparison, since Philip Gelvin, who appears as Babs's lover in the earlier book, reappears near the beginning of the later book, followed soon by the statement that another character in *Cartesian Sonata* is "thick through his thighs like Willie Masters' Lonesome Wife" (10). Yet, so of a piece is Gass's corpus that the comparison might have been made with any of Gass's earlier books of fiction. *Cartesian Sonata* does remind one of *Willie Masters' Lonesome Wife,* but no more than it reminds one of *The Tunnel* or *In the Heart of the Heart of the Country*. In fact, on the page after the reference to Willie Masters' Lonesome Wife, the speaker names William Frederick Kohler, and says he is "up on charges now for molesting his female students" (11).

The similarities do not stop at the characters. Explicit appeal to a musical form in the title and the echo of musical form in the title story resemble the reference to the twelve-tone scale in the structure of *The Tunnel*. The frequent allusions to and quotations of poetry throughout the book, especially in "Emma Enters a Sentence of Elizabeth Bishop's," recall the allusions to Rilke in "Order of Insects" and to

FOUR MOVEMENTS: *CARTESIAN SONATA*

Yeats in "In the Heart of the Heart of the Country." Family tensions familiar from the earlier works recur here, as do favorite elements like interiors, windows, and snow. Even so, each story includes some new aspect, beginning with clairvoyance in "Cartesian Sonata."

1. Cartesian Sonata

Her clairvoyance allows the main character, Ella Bend Hess, to function as a symbol of mind, making the "poisonous marriage" (so familiar from Gass's earlier fiction) into an allegory of mind versus matter, pitting "airy, clairvoyant Ella Bend Hess against her abusive Caliban of a husband, Edgar—mind and matter, recoiling from one another, yet inevitably knotted together in mutual complaint."[2] Structurally, the allegory has three parts, as sonata form dictates it must: the first "is narrated by the writer and concerns his difficulties with writing the story, the second is narrated from Ella's point of view, and third from her husband's as he watches over Ella during an illness."[3]

In the first section, the narrator admits no sympathy with the characters he has created, including Ella herself. "I hate her. I hate them all. That's not a manner of speaking. I have only to write down their names and I hate them. They make my stomach turn" (23). In saying so, the narrator expects his attitude to guide the reader, and the cue extends to all of Gass's fiction, since (with the possible exceptions of Jorge in "The Pedersen Kid," for whom one might feel sorry, and the protagonist in "Order of Insects," who seems to manifest goodwill) there are no characters with whom to identify or sympathize. All are distasteful in some way.

Instead of the snow that often serves as Gass's objective correlative for spiritual blankness, this narrator adopts dust. "It is August.

The roads are dry. There is a film of dust on everything. It settles slowly as the snow falls softly on my window. But dust is more enduring, stays the seasons, surfaces the wings of birds, persists through fiction, drifts from Ella Bend to me." Dust creates the environment in which, godlike and prophetically, "I shall write my mene mene tekel upharsin on her dining room table, my fingernail like the skate of a ghost" (23).[4]

In the second section, the point of view shifts away from the narrator toward Ella, with emphasis on the peculiar nature of her experience. For example: "Noises, I can see noises, she had once said to a neighbor, immediately regretting it" (28). In this synesthesia, her experience resembles that reported in psychological case studies, like that of the "mnemonist" studied by A. R. Luria, who reported that "every sound he heard immediately produced an experience of light and color" and "a sense of touch and taste as well."[5] In Ella's experience, "Everything leaves a wake" (34).

Ella's clairvoyance has haunted her as long as she can remember. "For a long time as a child she'd thought that everyone could see at night, in darkness, as well and easily as she could. She'd thought that when her mother laughed, everyone saw the needles, or the dark licorice stain that spread over her chest, sometimes, when she talked" (34). Naturally, she came to realize eventually that her experience was exceptional, and that she was not only perceiving differently than others, but *more* than others. Her world was charged with meaning: "Space wasn't space to Ella, it was signals" (36).

As with the mythical Cassandra (referred to early in the story), or the poet/courtier given a white elephant in Jack Gilbert's "In Dispraise of Poetry," whose gift "could not be refused,"[6] Ella recognizes her fatidical gift as also her curse. She goes to a psychic for

FOUR MOVEMENTS: *CARTESIAN SONATA*

help getting "rid of her gifts," but "Madame Betz was frightened and sent her away. Ella persisted, nevertheless. She came back again and again. Isn't there someone you could find who would like them—someone I could give them to, Ella begged." But Madame Betz replied that "your gifts aren't organs you can get dead and donate" (41). Ella's clairvoyance is the version of hyperawareness that makes her akin to Gass's other main characters: by giving her an overdeveloped attention and training it on aspects of the world important to her private experience, it makes her simultaneously closer to and more aware of the inhuman world, and more uncompromisingly isolated from other humans.

In the third section, Ella's husband, Edgar, gets his turn to have a say, and he doesn't like Ella's gift any more than she does. His imagined conversation with a doctor leads him to fantasize about eliminating her gift by eliminating her altogether. "You've no young children, I suppose, Hess, have you?" the imaginary doctor asks, "and I trust you're well insured. Ha ha, Mr. Hess thought. Ha ha. And he solemnly prayed for his wife's demise" without feeling guilt. "She was sick enough," he told himself, "to be lots better dead. That was a fact, god's truth. Hess wished her speedy passage o'er the great divide as he wished, weekends, for green golfing weather" (45).

His wish for her death arises from the disparity between their modes of being. She is almost pure spirit, and he almost pure body. He "knew no more of the spirit than his hat did" (46). Her gift meant that he was far too material for her, and she was not material enough for him. "There was no place or moment she was willing to occupy the way Hess took over his air and hours—fully, heavily, persistently—so he was unable to feel there were any outlines to her —no weights, no volumes, no shifts—she was never anywhere" (53).

Edgar, whose being is a body, knows how to respond to their dilemma only physically, so he makes theirs a life of "never touching except, like I've said, when I reach out and whack her," but physical violence cannot enforce reconciliation because she responds as any spirit would: "she knows days in advance—yes siree, no mistake—why, sometimes the bruise will be there, yellow and green like a young banana, days before the blow" (59).

Edgar, a body in a world Ella infuses with spirit, ends up a candidate for Kohler's Party of the Disappointed People: "Reality broke in like a burglar and stole his dreams before he could etch his name" (62). For her part, Ella, a spirit in a world Edgar weighs down with body, "has no defenses against the invasion of her brain by the world and everything in it," leaving "her unrestricted senses" no possibility but to "deplete the world's authenticity and specificity."[7]

2. Bed and Breakfast

Like "The Reverend Jethro Furber's Change of Heart" in *Omensetter's Luck,* "Bed and Breakfast" recounts the "change of heart" of a sleazy character. It describes Walter Riffaterre (Walt Riff as he is usually called, in another, somewhat less elevated musical reference to complement the book's title) as "a traveling cut-rate accountant" who "moved from town to town and firm to firm—little loose ones mostly, like buttons about to come off—and cooked books until their figures resembled fudge. He issued statements saying all was well, which it was when he got through erasing and rewriting" (73). He knows his work is illegal and immoral, but lacks the will to redirect his life. He is "Willy Loman in his youth,"[8] at a point where a meaningful change of heart still remains a real, if unlikely, possibility.

FOUR MOVEMENTS: *CARTESIAN SONATA*

Like Auntie in *The Tunnel,* Walt Riff insinuates himself into the lives of his employers, making himself indispensable. "Gradually, as these things usually happen, he became a fixer, somebody the corner store could count on, slow as mold but sure as rust. He would carry all kinds of blank receipts in his valise, and make up expenses, their lying numbers, like words for a story." But he does not stop with fudging a little here and there. "He didn't just juggle figures, he rebalanced lives, created costs and catastrophes, invented divorces, begot additional children" (76). Riff is a poet, a creator, but only the most corrupted, diminished sort, a financial pornographer who parodies Gass's criticism of pornography as "poor stuff, not because it promotes lascivious feelings, but because these feelings are released by and directed toward unreal things" (*FFL,* 284).

Every element in the story conspires to make the reader aware of Riff's increasing recognition of his own corruption. Even the name "Missus Ambrose" contributes to this effect. Ambrose was the bishop responsible for St. Augustine's conversion to Christianity, so this story (like *The Tunnel*) models itself on that prototypical conversion story, Augustine's *Confessions,* a "change of heart" that antedates Jethro Furber's and Walt Riff's by fifteen centuries. Mrs. Ambrose's first name is Bettie, short for Elizabeth, who was (according to the Gospel of Luke) the wife of the priest Zechariah and the mother of John the Baptist; if one could speak of a "conversion" or a "change of heart" in the Jesus of the gospels, it was John the Baptist who administered the sacrament attesting to it.

The characters conspire to make Riff aware of his baseness, but so does the house itself, which, even before Riff meets Mrs. Ambrose, heightens his consciousness of his corrupt nature. The house where Mr. and Mrs. Ambrose live symbolizes purity and salvation, appealing again to Christian religious narratives like the passage in which Jesus declares that "in my Father's house are many mansions." The walk leading to the house is described (in phrasing reminiscent of the Protestant hymn "Onward, Christian Soldiers") as being "made of evenly laid brick" that marches "straight to the house like a battalion on the move." All the visible parts of the house participate in the conspiracy, reminding Riff (and the narrator and the reader) of religious phenomena. "On the porch there were a swing and hanging pots. Its nicely spindled railing curled round a corner out of sight. Up on the second floor façade, dark green shutters were folded back against a wall of bright red bricks like a photograph for Christmas" (88–89). The suggestion of the house as paradise or heaven receives reinforcement at every step in the story, as when the narrator expresses Riff's judgment that "there was no place appropriate for pain here, it hurt to have hurts in this—sure, material—sure, commercial—although transient—heaven. Well, haven, anyway" (108).

Confronted with so firm an edifice of piety, Riff becomes "shamefaced" as soon as he steps on the porch, and his valise reminds him of his fallen state. "He held his valise up close to his chest, concealing the belt buckle, of which he had suddenly become very aware. But his case was scratched and crummy. A button on his shirt was a bit pulled" (89). The same contrast occurs repeatedly. "This room seemed to call for order. Try to be somebody for a change, his soul said," but then "the familiar suitcase sling with its crossed legs and standard straps," calls out to his shabby valise, which appears in its ordinariness "as out of place as Riff was, who had lit here like some bird blown off course" (102). The sentence's concluding simile summons yet another Christian commonplace: Jesus' assertion in the Sermon on the Mount that God cares for every sparrow.

FOUR MOVEMENTS: *CARTESIAN SONATA*

The house enforces a change in Riff. Before, he had depended on external, physical security—a verifiable measure taken—as indicated by the fact that he "always closed the door to the bathroom, even when alone, even when his room was safely chained and double-bolted" (70). In the bed and breakfast, protected by the house and tended to by Mrs. Ambrose, his sense of security becomes internal and spiritual—a feeling. He "was overwhelmed by the opulence which now enveloped him, a plenty which made him feel secure, embowered even—pillowed, draped, laced" in spite of his noticing, "as he closed it, that his door had no lock, no catch, no latch, no hook" (91). The physical surroundings contribute to Riff's security in part because they so transparently signify the spiritual, and Mrs. Ambrose contributes because in his perception she so steadfastly manifests the spiritual. He "felt the strength of her belief like a firm hand on his arm" (96).

Mrs. Ambrose holds to the Deuteronomic theology, that God rewards virtue and punishes vice, and cites her own husband as an example of the latter. "Mister Ambrose," she says, "pays the price. He has asthma, emphysema, and an artificial larynx. Oh . . . Oh dear. For every vice you pay a price, she recited" (99). In his desire to be redeemed from being "a bottom dealer and low roller and only a guy who made the vacancy sign go off" (115), Riff creates an idealized picture of Bettie's purity that starts with his own occupation, accounting, which he assumes she does carefully and justly. "Walter bet Bettie kept clean accounts. He bet she knew the date on every penny" (122). But his idealization also extends to his unacknowledged preoccupation, sex, in regard to which he "felt certain that sachets lay in her handkerchief drawers; that small scented pillows were being flattened by mattresses in all her beds; that she kept tussie-mussies too, deep in her purse; and that flexible stalks of lavender, plaited into dollies like his mother had once done corn, were tossed among her underthings like herbs in a salad" (122). In his mind, Bettie is pure through and through.

In the presence of a person so like the person he thinks he should be but knows he is not, he resolves to "make his soul work out as though it was some fatty in the gym. He would make himself measure up. Hadn't he stood in the doorway as a kid to have a line marked on the jamb where his head reached? It was his last chance to be Walter Riffaterre" (133). In support of that ambition, he nervously suggests a deal that would let him stay on, though "I can't afford the full fee, not right now at any rate," but "what I hoped was that maybe the longer stay—you see—would make possible a lesser price," and "I could always lend a hand around the house" (140). To his surprise, he sees that Mrs. Ambrose's "hand was shaking slightly" and her "gaze had grown watery." He adds the request that she recommend a church to him, and then has to try to hide his excitement when she agrees to the deal by saying, "Well, Mister Riffytear, that's a fine thought, since the season's slowing. And Mister could certainly use some help with the walk come snowtime. Let's just say a week for trial" (140).

The story closes, though, with his discovering something that draws into question his view of the place as paradise and of Mrs. Ambrose as its angel. Resolving to "take some steps toward a better future," he looks for a pad on which he can write names and addresses of prospective clients, but when he "grope[s] about" in the top desk drawer he pulls out a G-string. He wads it "in his fist as if to conceal it from himself, his face hot with shame and shock" (141–42). Among the religious artifacts and pious sayings, racy women's underwear was not what he expected to find. "The news that the world was ending would not have disturbed him half so much" (142). Like Wallace Stevens's jar on a hill in Tennessee that "made the slovenly wilderness / Surround that hill,"[9] the G-string changes everything in the room. Riff recognizes the items in the room as "all the other mementos" of the Ambrose's long-ago wedding, "all the bridal things" (142). He then sees the G-string as the satisfying completion of the decor in which "little messages" left everywhere "spoke through every detail, even in the deep corners of drawers, where some gesture shows up to say: the heart's been here and cared for even this little lost place; nothing has been neglected; nothing has been overlooked, nothing rejected" (143). The purity has washed over everything, even what is for him the prototypically impure. "Even this, Walter said in amazement, his face in the satin. Ummm . . . this. This too."

3. Emma Enters a Sentence . . .

Again in the collection's third novella, familiar patterns recur: reference to modernist poetry, a bleak midwestern landscape, a hyperprivate main character, and so on. The new presence in this story is anorexia. As her way of dealing with "her mother's indifference and her father's scorn,"[10] the main character, Emma, "was living off her body the way some folks were once said to live off the land." Emma takes quite literally Socrates' preference for soul over body, and his corollary that lovers of wisdom "make dying their profession." She seeks to make herself wholly spiritual and linguistic, and therefore insubstantial, immaterial. "She would grow thin enough, she thought, to slip into a sentence of the poet's like a spring frock" (147).

The familiar elements of the story begin with the house, isolated and decaying. "Emma owned an Iowa house," inherited from her parents, "empty and large and cool in the fall. Otherwise inhospitable. It had thin windows with wide views, a kitchen with counters of scrubbed wood, a woodshed built of now wan boards, a weakly sagging veranda, weedy yard" (147). Her careless neglect of the house, that square, once-sturdy body to which she is wholly indifferent, contrasts with her studied neglect of her own body. Her neglect of the house is passive, but her neglect of her body is active, resulting from "her decision to lie down in a line of verse and be buried there; that is to say, to be born again as a simple set of words" (148). The house can decay into she-cares-not-what, but she wants her body to become something very specific.

The house extends into a landscape made mythical by allusion to familiar biblical narratives, first the Garden of Eden. Instead of an apple tree in the middle of the garden, an ash tree near the house "sucked all the water from the ground and shaded a wide round circle too where nothing much grew," symbolizing the corruption of the land: "'This is the tree Satan's snake spoke from,' Emma's father would say, his tone as certain as gospel. 'It is the dirtiest tree on God's earth.' The risen emblem of a fallen world" (166). The tree's connection with Eden continues, when one day, as Emma sat "upon a smooth bare root, her back against the trunk," she is surprised: "a branch, broken in a previous storm but caught by other branches, slipped out of their grasp and fell like a spear, stabbing her ankle with such a suddenness she screamed, feeling snake-bit" (167). In case the reader misses that way of marking the corruption of the land, Gass connects it with another biblical garden that is the site of corruption, the Garden of Gethsemane (where Christ was betrayed by Judas), by

FOUR MOVEMENTS: *CARTESIAN SONATA*

having Emma cry, "not from pain or even shock, but because she'd been betrayed" (167).

The now familiar references to modernist poetry cite, as the title indicates, the work of Elizabeth Bishop. In some cases, the references are made explicit (either by being set off in the text or identified as quotations), but sometimes not. For example, at one point Emma says, "I have lost this, lost that, am I not an expert at it?" (152), alluding to Bishop's villanelle entitled "The Art of Losing." The same poem reappears later in the story, but this time the first line of the poem is directly quoted: "The art of losing isn't hard to master" (161). Another example occurs when the narrator reports that "the world was a mist and black figures slowly emerged from the mist" (159). The wording there draws on Bishop's poem "Sandpiper," which describes the shore bird looking for food as the tide comes in and out: "The world is a mist. And then the world is / minute and vast and clear."[11] Such references pepper the story, as they must; if Emma has entered a sentence of Elizabeth Bishop's, Bishop's sentences will inevitably enter Emma's story.

As for the new element in this story, Emma's anorexia, the blame for it is laid on her parents, especially her father, who attends carefully to, and comments lewdly on, her physical development. In *Willie Masters' Lonesome Wife,* Babs's father had praised the ampleness of her breasts: "There was never any doubt about my bosom, buddy.... A regular dairy, my daddy always said." In "Emma Enters a Sentence," however, the father's comments, though similarly focused on the size of the daughter's developing breasts, are inappropriate insults instead of inappropriate praise. "My father would stare at my bony body. Shake his head sadly. Nothing there to raise a dick. I'd be bare. Stand there. Bedsided. Scared. Oh yes mortified. Ashamed" (152).

Her father's frustration, which he takes out on her, has built up in part because the transition to farm life exemplifies a misunderstanding of his own nature. "Her father really should have kept the grease beneath his nails and never replaced it with plant smutch and field dirt. His world was mechanical, not organic" (169). For her part, Emma is organic, not mechanical, so his general lack of sympathy with the organic entails a lack of sympathy with her.

Like her father, Emma's mother manages to damage her, but if her father harms Emma by his activity, her mother harms her by her passivity. Always ill, she "took her sturdy time dying," and in the meantime paid no attention to Emma. She was "married to a gangplank of a guy. She scarcely spoke to me. I think she was ashamed of the way she let him make me live" (153). Like Emma, her mother grows increasingly insubstantial as a way of responding to Emma's father. Neither body satisfies him, or is satisfied by him, so each wastes away. Emma herself "was a residue, her life as the light in her inherited house," and her mother "had died in the bed she had no doubt grown to loathe, a bed full of him every night until her illness drove him out, lying there in a knot, staring up through the dark at death—who would not want it to come quick?" (157). The daughter chooses a different illness, but still drives him out.

Emma feels condemned to repeat her mother's despair: "her life would be like her mother's just the same. They'd endure until they died. That would be it," not only because she feels herself unable to choose any other course, but because she sees no other course to choose. "Over the world, as far as she could see, that was it" (159). Through an ironic reversal, though, her bodily starvation becomes spiritual nourishment. She and her mother and her father had each "hungered for the others' deaths. Now Emma was fed" (172).

4. The Master of Secret Revenges

"The Master of Secret Revenges" continues *Cartesian Sonata*'s exploration of religious themes, and fits well as the final story to be studied in a book on William Gass's work, because it "stands as perhaps the best short example (*The Tunnel* is the longest) of the author's love of mixing high and low, philosophy and farts, Manichaeanism and masturbation."[12] It is the story of one Luther Penner, who maintains it as his "solemn purpose to improve on Nature and prefigure Providence" (192), at whatever cost to himself.

Penner, like some of Gass's other characters, is preoccupied with the problem of evil: that there appears to be no correlation between the worth of a person's actions and the quality of her or his circumstances. The world seems not to reward good actions or punish bad ones. In Gerard Manley Hopkins's formulation, the question is, "Why do sinners' ways prosper? and why must / Disappointment all I endeavour end?"[13] The attraction Mrs. Ambrose holds for Riff in "Bed and Breakfast" derives from her creating an environment that sanctions his believing, as she so obstinately does, that the world *does* reward good actions and punish bad ones; and Kohler's bitterness in *The Tunnel,* his passive disappointment, follows from his belief that the world neither rewards good nor punishes bad, and that he can do nothing to remedy the situation.

Penner is "interested in mixing the ingratiation of wishful thinking with the criticality of knowing better,"[14] in pursuing a course between Mrs. Ambrose's and Kohler's, neither to retreat into the delusion that the world is fair, nor to throw up his hands and accept its unfairness. Penner undertakes a reformation. "Like his famous namesake, Luther would reform us in everything" (193). If the world is unjust, he will try to alter it. The method Penner adopts for reform is the secret revenge, which he believes "puts within the reach of every ordinary man and woman a truly formidable weapon which balances at once the forces of the weakling with the bully's, and one which must, in time, surely tip the scales to the nobler side" (193). Secrecy makes Penner's system an inversion of the Gyges ring story in Plato: there, the shepherd's secrecy (in the form of invisibility) frees him to do unjust actions; Penner expects secrecy to further actions he considers just.

The narrator posits an origin for Luther's ideas. "It is possible," he says, "that Penner's conception of a pure revenge reflected his father's habit of swearing in secret, damning images, and cursing a commentator who existed only as a voice" (197–98). If so, then Penner embodies Nietzsche's aperçu, "what was silent in the father speaks in the son,"[15] and Penner resembles other Gass characters, from Jorge through Kohler, who define their stances toward life on the basis of bitterness toward their parents.

Luther's idea of the secret revenge is based on the principle of *lex talionis*. "The punishment should be suitable to the crime—like an iron maiden, cut to fit—that was the ancient principle, and properly interpreted, it would certainly prove itself over and over again" (199). Penner's writings affirm that "An eye for an eye is the only moral law" (209), and he tries to make himself the agent who enforces that law, by undertaking a series of secret revenges, some more successful than others, but from each of which he learns some lesson to guide him in the next.

Early on, for example, the narrator describes Luther's frustration as a boy at being made to help his Aunt Spatz with household chores, and the revenge he attempts by drying the silver with used, unlaundered socks; from which revenge he learns to calculate consequences,

FOUR MOVEMENTS: *CARTESIAN SONATA*

since it left him with the likelihood he himself would have to eat on his next visit with a fork he had "treated." His revenges against the three school bullies, Cy, Syph, and Larry, show more forethought, as when he takes a drink before recess and holds the water in his cheek, so that spitting on the boy who punches him will appear involuntary and not provoke further punching.

Penner's revenges continue through his youth, with the lack of subtlety one expects from an adolescent: peeing into the gas tank of a delivery van owned by a company from which he was fired, for example. As he ages, his revenges become more complex. For instance, he responds to the flood of mail-order catalogs by sending to the catalog companies "packaged dried dog turds tied together like small logs with a ribbon and a message which read: *you send me shit I don't want; I send you shit you don't want*" (219). The preoccupation with excrement recurs in many of his revenges, notably in his revenge on Professor Hoch for a perceived slight, accomplished by pissing in Hoch's desk drawer.

The excremental theme embodies one of Penner's principles. "Just as the body is soiled by the excrement it makes and carries, so the soul, you see, is blackened by its dirty deeds, hence the appropriateness of using bodily fluids as punishments—spitting on faces fastened in the stocks, for instance—because punishment is always levied against the body, isn't it, even when it is the inner character—the spirit—that commits the crime" (254). To propagate that principle, Penner pens "An Immodest Proposal," which proposes punishing criminals by locking them in "piss pits" located in public places and designed so that passersby "might pee on the deserving wretch below" (251).

Penner meets an ignominious end in what the narrator speculates may have been a secret revenge gone wrong, but if the aspect of his death sets him apart from other Gass characters, in other respects he represents them. He typifies Gass characters in his scatological preoccupation, his resentment and bitterness, his unhappy childhood, and his sense that he "was a superior person forced to lead an inferior life" (203). Robert Browning's poems epitomize the optimism that the distance by which one's reach exceeds one's grasp signifies the hope of heaven; William Gass's fiction epitomizes the pessimism that the distance by which one's reach exceeds one's grasp makes one's life a very hell.

NOTES

Chapter 1—Understanding William H. Gass

1. Gass, "'Nothing but Darkness and Talk?': Writers' Symposium on Traditional Values and Iconoclastic Fiction," *Critique* 31, no. 4 (summer 1990): 240. Substituting "the page for the world," Gass says in the same paragraph, is a form of revenge for the recognition that "you are, in terms of the so-called world, an impotent nobody."

2. Gass, *A Temple of Texts: Fifty Literary Pillars* (St. Louis: Olin Library, Washington University, 1991), 28.

3. Czeslaw Milosz, *Nobel Lecture* (New York: Farrar Straus Giroux, 1981), 20.

4. Elias Canetti, *Crowds and Power,* trans. Carol Stewart (New York: Farrar Straus Giroux, 1984), 306.

5. Gass recalls his father's nostalgic stories of his baseball career in "'Spit in the Mitt': Father, Son, and Baseball," *Student Life* (Washington University student newspaper), 12 April 1994.

6. Marie Arana-Ward, "William H. Gass," *Washington Post Book World,* 24 November 1996, 10.

7. In Thomas LeClair, "Interview with William Gass," in *Anything Can Happen: Interviews with Contemporary American Novelists* (Urbana: University of Illinois Press, 1983), 154–55.

8. In G. A. M. Janssens, "An Interview with William Gass," *Dutch Quarterly Review* 9, no. 4 (1979): 259.

9. Ibid., 242–43.

10. In Ildikó Kaposi, "A Talk with William H. Gass," *Hungarian Journal of English and American Studies* 3, no. 1 (1997): 17.

11. In Lorna Domke, "An Interview with William Gass," *Missouri Review* 10, no. 3 (1987): 66. Gass's happiest time, he reports in the same

interview, came not long after his second marriage, when he and his wife lived for six months in Portugal, sponsored by a Guggenheim grant.

12. In LeClair, "Interview with William Gass," 156.

13. In Kaposi, "A Talk with William H. Gass," 9.

14. In Janssens, "An Interview with William Gass," 247.

15. In Carole Spearin McCauley, "Fiction Needn't Say Things—It Should Make Them out of Words: An Interview with William H. Gass," in *The New Fiction: Interviews with Innovative American Writers,* ed. Joe David Bellamy (Urbana: University of Illinois Press, 1975), 44. Gass claims to go through so many drafts that in effect he works "not by writing but by rewriting."

16. Gass sometimes reports having begun *The Tunnel* in 1965 (e.g., Bonetti recording) and sometimes in 1966 (e.g., McCauley, 45); in either case, of course, it was nearly thirty years in the making.

Chapter 2—Four Characters in *Omensetter's Luck*

1. In LeClair, "Interview with William Gass," 169.

2. Arthur Saltzman, "Where Words Dwell Adored: An Introduction to William Gass," *Review of Contemporary Fiction* 11, no. 3 (fall 1991): 8.

3. In LeClair, "Interview with William Gass," 172. Earlier in the same interview, Gass reports that Furber's importance increased as the book was rewritten. "When I first wrote the book, Furber wasn't even in it." But that manuscript was stolen from his office, so Gass rewrote the book, and "it was then that Furber began to emerge."

4. Gass, "A Letter to the Editor," in *Afterwords: Novelists on Their Novels,* ed. Thomas McCormack (New York: Harper & Row, 1969), 95–96.

5. Richard J. Schneider, "Rejecting the Stone: William Gass and Emersonian Transcendence," *Review of Contemporary Fiction* 11, no. 3 (fall 1991): 122.

NOTES TO PAGES 8–18

6. Saltzman, *The Fiction of William Gass: The Consolation of Language* (Carbondale: Southern Illinois University Press, 1986), 26.

7. Aristotle, *Poetics,* trans. Ingram Bywater, in *The Basic Works of Aristotle,* ed. Richard McKeon (New York: Random House, 1941), 1452a.

8. Larry McCaffery, *The Metafictional Muse: The Works of Robert Coover, Donald Barthelme, and William H. Gass* (Pittsburgh: University of Pittsburgh Press, 1982), 225–26.

9. McCaffery, *The Metafictional Muse,* 225.

10. Gass, "A Letter to the Editor," 97.

11. Schneider, Richard J. "The Fortunate Fall in William Gass's *Omensetter's Luck,*" *Critique* 18, no. 1 (summer 1976): 120.

12. Saltzman, *The Fiction of William Gass,* 33.

13. Gass, "A Letter to the Editor," 96.

14. Schneider, "The Fortunate Fall," 120 (emphasis added).

15. The identification of Omensetter with water continues throughout Pimber's section. For example, the narrator comments that Omensetter's hands "added themselves to what they touched, enlarging them, as rivers meet and magnify their stream" (41).

16. Saltzman, *The Fiction of William Gass,* 37.

17. McCaffery, *The Metafictional Muse,* 233.

18. Gass, "A Letter to the Editor," 98.

19. Ibid.

20. Schneider, "The Fortunate Fall," 10.

21. McCaffery, *The Metafictional Muse,* 234.

22. Saltzman, *The Fiction of William Gass,* 41.

23. Kay Ryan, "Full Measure," in *Elephant Rocks* (New York: Grove Press, 1996), 14.

24. Schneider, "Rejecting the Stone: William Gass and Emersonian Transcendence," *Review of Contemporary Fiction* 11, no. 3 (fall 1991): 121.

25. "The Marriage of Heaven and Hell," in *The Complete Poetry and Prose of William Blake,* ed. David V. Erdman (New York: Doubleday, 1988), 35.

26. McCaffery, *The Metafictional Muse,* 246.

27. Jean-Jacques Rousseau, *Émile,* trans. Allan Bloom (New York: Basic Books, 1979), 80.

28. Gass, "A Letter to the Editor," 94.

29. In Jo Brans, "Games of the Extremes," *Southwest Review* 70, no. 4 (autumn 1985): 448. The quoted words are Gass's, except for the phrase "making love with words," which is suggested by the interviewer and then affirmed by Gass.

30. Gass, "A Letter to the Editor," 102.

31. Carolyn J. Allen, "Fiction and Figures of Life in *Omensetter's Luck,*" *Pacific Coast Philology* 9 (April 1974): 7.

32. Ibid., 9–10.

33. In the interview that constitutes chapter 7 of Saltzman's *The Fiction of William Gass,* 156.

34. McCaffery, *The Metafictional Muse,* 228.

35. Although the identification with Claudius is implicit here, the novel's narrator makes it explicit later, when he includes in Furber's interior monologue the sentences, "O-men-set-ter. Now his name has entered his ear. In whose porches I poured the poison" (202), which echoes King Hamlet's ghost's testament that "in the porches of my ear" Claudius "did pour / The leperous distilment" of poison. The echo is repeated on page 232.

36. Margaret Dornfeld, "Gass's *Omensetter's Luck,*" *Explicator* 39, no. 4 (summer 1981): 43.

37. Watson L. Holloway, *William Gass* (Boston: Twayne, 1990), 30.

38. Saltzman, *The Fiction of William Gass,* 52.

39. Schneider, "Rejecting the Stone," 120.

40. Saltzman, *The Fiction of William Gass,* 48.

41. James McCourt, "Fiction in Review," *Yale Review* 83, no 3 (July 1995): 159–69.

42. This is not the only parallel between *Omensetter's Luck* and *Hamlet.* For example, Watson L. Holloway observes that "just as the

rather loose and farfetched plot of *Hamlet* serves as mere scaffolding for the rhetorical vigor of the prince's monologues, Gass's novel weaves its episodic convolutions into a central platform for the discourse of the Reverend Jethro Furber" (18).

43. *Anatomy of Criticism* (Princeton, N.J.: Princeton University Press, 1957), 207.

44. In LeClair, "Interview with William Gass," 164. He reiterates the point in autobiographical rather than literary-critical terms in another interview: "I, of course, have never been, except to drive through, in an Ohio rivertown. I chose that part of the world precisely because I knew nothing about it. I wanted to be able, really, to create something and not to worry about being accurate." Brooke K. Horvath et al., "A Colloquy with William H. Gass," *Modern Fiction Studies* 29, no. 4 (winter 1983): 589.

45. In McCauley, "Fiction Needn't Say Things," 39.

46. "Mississippi," *Yale Review* 83, no. 1 (January 1995): 1.

47. W. S. Merwin, trans., *Asian Figures* (New York: Atheneum, 1973), 35.

48. Holloway, *William Gass,* 39.

Chapter 3—Five Stories: *In the Heart of the Heart of the Country*

1. Aristotle, *Poetics,* trans. Ingram Bywater, in *The Basic Works of Aristotle,* ed. Richard McKeon (New York: Random House, 1941), 1450a. Aristotle speaks specifically of tragedy; I have extended his case to all narratives.

2. Holloway, *William Gass,* 47.

3. Saltzman, *The Fiction of William Gass,* 57–58.

4. Marcus Klein, quoted in Ray Lewis White, "The Early Fiction of William H. Gass: A Critical Documentary," *Midamerica* 7 (1979): 175–76.

5. Ludwig Wittgenstein, *Tractatus Logico-Philosophicus,* trans. D. F. Pears and B. F. McGuinness (London: Routledge & Kegan Paul, 1961). The quoted passages are 5.61 and 5.632, respectively.

NOTES TO PAGES 33–44

6. Tony Tanner, "William Gass's Barns and Bees," *Scenes of Nature, Signs of Men* (Cambridge: Cambridge University Press, 1987), 258.

7. Kevin J. H. Dettmar, "'yung and easily freudened': William Gass's 'The Pedersen Kid,'" *Review of Contemporary Fiction* 11, no. 3 (fall 1991): 88–89.

8. Ibid., 93.

9. Ibid., 94.

10. Melanie Eckford-Prossor, "Layered Apparitions: Philosophy and 'The Pedersen Kid,'" *Review of Contemporary Fiction* 11, no. 3 (fall 1991): 106.

11. Saltzman, *The Fiction of William Gass*, 64.

12. Patricia Kane, "The Sun Burned on the Snow: Gass's 'The Pedersen Kid,'" *Critique* 14, no. 2 (1972): 90.

13. Holloway, *William Gass*, 57.

14. Bruce Bassoff, "The Sacrificial World of William Gass: *In the Heart of the Heart of the Country*," *Critique* 18, no. 1 (summer 1976): 42, 44.

15. Friedrich Nietzsche, *The Will to Power*, trans. Walter Kaufmann and R. J. Hollingdale (New York: Vintage, 1968), 135.

16. Reginald Dyck, "William Gass: A 'Purified Modernist' in a Postmodern World," *Review of Contemporary Fiction* 11, no. 3 (fall 1991): 129.

17. T. S. Eliot, *Collected Poems, 1909–1962* (New York: Harcourt, Brace & World, 1970), 57–58.

18. Ibid., 7.

19. Gass himself translates the line "Who, if I cried, would hear me among the Dominions / of Angels?" (*RR*, 189). To capture better the connection between "Order of Insects" and the original German "Engel Ordnungen," the translation in the text more closely approximates the earliest versions quoted in the comparative list Gass compiles on page 57 of *Reading Rilke*.

20. Eusebio L. Rodrigues, "A Nymph at Her Orisons: An Analysis of William Gass's 'Order of Insects,'" *Studies in Short Fiction* 17, no. 3 (summer 1980): 348.

21. Schneider, "Rejecting the Stone," 118.

22. Vanessa Haley, "Egyptology and Entomology in William Gass's 'Order of Insects,'" *Notes on Contemporary Literature* 16 (May 1986): 3.

23. Saltzman, *The Fiction of William Gass,* 91.

24. The anal observer was Larry McCaffery, who wrote that "the story's thirty-six individual sections . . . correspond to the thirty-six lines in Yeats's poem" (*The Metafictional Muse,* 216).

25. In James McKenzie, "Pole-Vaulting in Top Hats: A Public Conversation with John Barth, William Gass, and Ishmael Reed," *Modern Fiction Studies* 22, no. 2 (summer 1976): 147.

26. In LeClair, "Interview with William Gass," 164.

27. Charlotte Byrd Hadella, "The Winter Wasteland of William Gass's 'In the Heart of the Heart of the Country,'" *Critique* 30, no. 1 (fall 1988): 49–50.

28. Frederick Busch, "But This Is What It Is Like to Live in Hell: William Gass's *In the Heart of the Heart of the Country,*" *Modern Fiction Studies* 19, no. 1 (spring 1973): 99.

Chapter 4—One Theme in Three Essays

1. Elizabeth W. Bruss, *Beautiful Theories: The Spectacle of Discourse in Contemporary Criticism.* (Baltimore: Johns Hopkins University Press, 1982), 139.

2. Rainer Maria Rilke, *Letters to a Young Poet,* trans. M. D. Herter Norton (New York: W. W. Norton, 1954), 29–30.

3. Gass, *New Letters on the Air* radio interview, 1990.

4. Immanuel Kant, *Critique of Pure Reason,* trans. Werner S. Pluhar (Indianapolis: Hackett, 1996), 21.

5. Larry McCaffery, "The Gass-Gardner Debate: Showdown on Main Street," *Literary Review* 23, no. 1 (fall 1979): 144.

6. Each of the six elements receives only a cursory examination in this essay, but each receives richer treatment in some other essay by Gass: perception in "The Anatomy of Mind" (*WWW*), emotion in "The Doomed in Their Sinking" (*WWW*), thought in "Representation and the War for Reality" (*HW*), speech in "On Talking to Oneself" (*HW*), desire in "The Stylization of Desire" (*FFL*), and imagination in "The Origin of Extermination in the Imagination" (*HW*).

7. C. S. Lewis, *The Discarded Image* (Cambridge: Cambridge University Press, 1964), 214.

8. Kant, *Grounding for the Metaphysics of Morals,* in *Immanuel Kant: Ethical Philosophy,* trans. James W. Ellington (Indianapolis, Ind.: Hackett, 1983), 36. The analogy makes particular sense if one views Kant as formalism's father.

Chapter 5—Two Shades of Blue: *Willie Masters' Lonesome Wife* and *On Being Blue*

1. In LeClair, "Interview with William Gass," 158.

2. Gass, "On Experimental Writing: Some Clues for the Clueless." *New York Times Book Review,* 21 August 1994, 3.

3. David Hayman, "Surface Disorders/Grave Disturbances," *TriQuarterly* 52 (fall 1981): 191.

4. In McCauley, "Fiction Needn't Say Things," 42.

5. McCaffery, *The Metafictional Muse,* 173.

6. The Dalkey Archive reprint uses white paper throughout, instead of replicating the various colors of paper used in the original *TriQuarterly* edition.

7. Holloway, *William Gass,* 79.

8. Marc Chénetier, *Beyond Suspicion: New American Fiction since 1960,* trans. Elizabeth A. Houlding (Philadelphia: University of Pennsylvania Press, 1996), 81–82.

9. Bruss, *Beautiful Theories,* 153–54.

10. Charles Caramello, "Fleshing Out *Willie Masters' Lonesome Wife,*" *Sub-Stance* 27 (1980): 59. Shakespeare spent the duration of his theatrical career (as actor, writer, and theater owner) in London, while his wife remained in Stratford, and scholars have long speculated over his *will,* which leaves to his wife only "the second-best bed."

11. Ibid., 60.

12. E. M. Cioran, *Anathemas and Admirations,* trans. Richard Howard (New York: Arcade, 1991), 106.

13. Frederick R. Karl, *American Fictions, 1940–1980: A Comprehensive History and Critical Evaluation* (New York: Harper & Row, 1983), 437.

14. Bruss, *Beautiful Theories*, 167–68.

15. In LeClair, "Interview with William Gass," 160.

16. In Jeffrey L. Duncan, "A Conversation with Stanley Elkin and William H. Gass," *Iowa Review* 7, no. 1 (winter 1976): 64.

17. Melanie Eckford-Prossor, "Shattering Genre/Creating Self: William Gass's *On Being Blue.*" *Style* 23, no. 2 (summer 1989): 280. The following overviews of each section of *On Being Blue* will take their initial direction by citing Eckford-Prossor's excellent analysis.

18. Ibid., 280.

19. Friedrich Nietzsche, *Daybreak,* trans. R. J. Hollingdale (Cambridge: Cambridge University Press, 1982), 145.

20. Eckford-Prossor, "Shattering Genre/Creating Self," 281.

21. Ibid.

22. Ibid., 293.

23. Gass, in Domke, "An Interview with William Gass," 56–57.

Chapter 6—Twenty Questions on *The Tunnel*

1. In McCauley, "Fiction Needn't Say Things," 44. "*The Tunnel,*" Gass says in the same paragraph, "is a crucial work for me."

NOTES TO PAGES 76–85

2. Quoted in Richard Byrne, "Notes from Underground," *Riverfront Times* 855, 22–28 February 1995, 19.

3. In Kaposi, "A Talk with William H. Gass," 17.

4. In Jo Brans, "Games of the Extremes," *Southwest Review* 70, no. 4 (autumn 1985): 443.

5. In McCauley, "Fiction Needn't Say Things," 45. Or, in another formulation, originally written about *Omensetter's Luck,* but surely applicable to *The Tunnel* as well, "this book was not written to have readers. It was written to *not* have readers, while still deserving them" (William Gass, "A Letter to the Editor," 105).

6. Michael Silverblatt, "A Small Apartment in Hell," *Los Angeles Times Book Review,* 19 March 1995, 1.

7. Robert Alter, "The Leveling Wind," *New Republic* 212, no. 13, 27 March 1995, 29.

8. Sven Birkerts, "One for the Angry White Male," *Atlantic Monthly* 275, no. 6 (June 1995): 114.

9. Steven G. Kellman and Irving Malin, eds. *Into "The Tunnel" : Readings of Gass's Novel* (Newark: University of Delaware Press, 1998), 9.

10. www.centerforbookculture.org. All quotations from the Barron, Eckford-Prossor, Barloon, and Di Blasi essays come from the casebook.

11. Gass, "The Test of Time," *Alaska Quarterly Review* 15, nos. 3 & 4 (spring & summer 1997): 83.

12. "'Nothing but Darkness and Talk?'" 241.

13. "There Was an Old Woman Who," in *Rewriting History,* ed. Heide Ziegler (Stuttgart: M & P Verlag, 1997), 95.

14. "Monumentality/Mentality," *Oppositions* 25 (fall 1982): 143.

15. In LeClair, "Interview with William Gass," 170.

16. Lynne McFall, *Happiness* (New York: Peter Lang, 1989), 57–77.

17. A Rwandan saying, quoted not by McFall, but in Canetti's *Notes from Hampstead,* trans. John Hargraves (New York: Farrar, Straus and Giroux, 1998), 22.

18. Frederick Seidel, *Poems, 1959–1979* (New York: Alfred A. Knopf, 1989), 81.

19. E. J. Cullen, *Our War and How We Won It* (New York: Viking, 1987), 7.

20. Canetti, *Notes from Hampstead,* 75.

21. John Leonard, "Splendor in the Gass?" *The Nation* 260, no. 11 (20 March 1995): 388.

22. In "'Nothing but Darkness and Talk?'" 247. Gass recommends indulging and then dismissing deconstruction, which was "interesting for a few minutes; now it's boring. We'll have something else."

23. Jean-François Lyotard, *The Postmodern Condition* (Minneapolis: University of Minnesota Press, 1984), 74.

24. Paul Mann, *Masocriticism* (Albany: State University of New York Press, 1999), 4.

25. Gass makes the statements about Kellerman and Richardson both in the Kaposi interview, "A Talk with William H. Gass," 13.

26. Gass, "A Case of Sincerity and Obsession," *New Republic* (23 September 1981): 27. Emphasis added.

27. James W. Tuttleton, "The Fascist Within?" *Washington Times,* 26 February 1995, B8.

28. René Descartes, *Discourse on Method,* in *The Philosophical Works of Descartes,* vol. 1, trans. Elizabeth S. Haldane and G. R. T. Ross (Cambridge: Cambridge University Press, 1931), 82.

29. For a full account of "satirical schizoscription," see H. L. Hix, *Morte d'Author: An Autopsy* (Philadelphia: Temple University Press, 1990), chapter 8.

30. *A Temple of Texts,* 47.

31. Edgar Allan Poe, "The Philosophy of Composition," in *Edgar Allan Poe: Selected Writings,* ed. David Galloway (New York: Penguin, 1967), 482.

32. In Jan Garden Castro, untitled interview with Gass, *Bomb* 51 (spring 1995): 60.

33. Antonio Porchia, *Voices,* trans. W. S. Merwin (New York: Alfred A. Knopf, 1988), 6.

34. Iris Murdoch, *Metaphysics as a Guide to Morals* (New York: Penguin, 1993), 258.

35. In Castro, untitled interview with Gass, 60.

36. "In the Dark Chambers of the Soul," *Washington Post Book World,* 12 March 1995, 10.

37. From an unpublished synopsis of *The Tunnel,* in the collection of Gass's papers at the International Writers Center, Washington University, St. Louis.

38. Ovid, *Metamorphoses,* trans. Rolfe Humphries (Bloomington: Indiana University Press, 1955): 236.

39. Plato, *Republic,* trans. G. M. A. Grube, rev. C. D. C. Reeve, in *Plato: Complete Works,* ed. John M. Cooper (Indianapolis: Hackett, 1997). This and the immediately following quotations from Plato come from the beginning of book 7.

40. Heide Ziegler, "William H. Gass: Is There Light at the End of *The Tunnel?* " in *Into "The Tunnel,"* ed. Kellman and Malin, 75.

41. Ludwig Wittgenstein, *Philosophical Investigations,* trans. G. E. M. Anscombe (New York: Macmillan, 1958), 203e.

42. Philip Graham, "This Way to the Abyss," *Chicago Tribune Books,* 5 March 1995, 5.

43. Simone Weil, *Gravity and Grace,* trans. Arthur Wills (Lincoln: University of Nebraska Press, 1997), 144.

44. Albert Camus, *The Myth of Sisyphus,* trans. Justin O'Brien (New York: Vintage Books, 1955), 89–90.

45. Søren Kierkegaard, *Stages on Life's Way,* ed. and trans. Howard V. Hong and Edna H. Hong (Princeton, N.J.: Princeton University Press, 1988), 248.

46. As Debra Di Blasi does in her essay in H. L. Hix, *A Casebook on "The Tunnel."*

47. Robert Kelly, "A Repulsively Lonely Man," *New York Times Book Review,* 26 February 1995, 18.

48. Louis Menand, "Journey into the Dark," *New York Review of Books,* 13 July 1995, 8. Gass himself recognizes that "I regularly run the risk of being said to have the same views that my narrator does" (Kaposi, "A Talk with William H. Gass," 12).

49. Alter, "A Leveling Wind," 31.

50. In Ziegler, "William H. Gass," 17.

51. Holloway, *William Gass,* 106.

52. Frank McConnell, "Alas, Gargantua," *Boston Sunday Globe,* 26 February 1995, B16.

53. Saltzman, *The Fiction of William Gass,* 126.

54. Wallace Stevens, "Adagia," in *Opus Posthumous* (New York: Vintage, 1982), 174.

55. Ibid., 163.

56. William Shakespeare, *The Third Part of King Henry the Sixth* 3.2.191–93. When he speaks these words, he is still the Duke of Gloucester, scheming to *become* Richard III.

57. Shakespeare, *Coriolanus* 3.3.124–27.

58. Kelly, "A Repulsively Lonely Man," 18.

59. Holloway, *William Gass,* 97–98.

60. Silverblatt, "A Small Apartment in Hell," 1. Emphasis added.

61. Merle Rubin, "Notes from a Postmodern 'Underground Man,'" *Christian Science Monitor,* 6 March 1995, 13.

62. David Hume, *A Treatise of Human Nature* (Oxford: Oxford University Press, 1978), 413.

63. Porchia, *Voices,* 33.

64. Murdoch, *Metaphysics as a Guide to Morals,* 103.

65. Holloway, *William Gass,* 102.

66. Percy Bysshe Shelley, "Defense of Poetry," in *Major British Poets of the Romantic Period*, ed. William Heath (New York: Macmillan, 1973), 978.

67. Canetti, *Notes from Hampstead,* 106.

68. Ralph Waldo Emerson, "History," in *Ralph Waldo Emerson: Essays and Journals,* ed. Lewis Mumford (Garden City, N.Y.: Doubleday, 1968), 72.

69. Aristotle, trans. Ingram Bywater, in *The Basic Works of Aristotle,* trans. Richard McKeon (New York: Random House, 1941), 1451b.

70. Emerson, "History," 72.

71. Holloway, *William Gass,* 99.

72. "There Was an Old Woman Who," 84

73. Ibid., 99. Emphasis added.

74. Gass, "The Test of Time," 75–76.

75. Weil, *Gravity and Grace,* 229.

76. Saint Augustine, *The Confessions of St. Augustine,* trans. Rex Warner (New York: New American Library, 1963), 45, 50.

77. In Ziegler, "William H. Gass," 16.

78. Giacomo Leopardi, *Pensieri,* trans. W. S. Di Piero (Oxford: Oxford University Press, 1984), 65.

79. James Wolcott, "Gass Attack," *New Criterion* 13, no. 6 (February 1995): 65.

80. Stevens, "Adagia," 161.

81. In Duncan, "A Conversation with Stanley Elkin and William H. Gass," 51.

82. Steven Moore, Review of *The Tunnel, Review of Contemporary Fiction* 15, no. 1 (1995): 159.

83. James Bowman, "The Tunnel," *National Review* 47, no. 8 (1 May 1995): 82.

84. Gass, "How German Are We?" *German Politics and Society* 13, no. 3 (fall 1995): 170.

85. Unpublished synopsis of *The Tunnel,* in the collection of Gass's papers at the International Writers Center, Washington University, St. Louis.

NOTES TO PAGES 138–153

86. Eudora Welty, *One Writer's Beginnings* (Cambridge: Harvard University Press, 1984), 69.

87. Meir Sternberg, *The Poetics of Biblical Narrative* (Bloomington: Indiana University Press, 1985), 50–51.

Chapter 7—Four Movements: *Cartesian Sonata*

1. Steven Moore, "Maestro of the Language," *Washington Post Book World,* 20 September 1998, 5.

2. Saltzman, Review of *Cartesian Sonata, Review of Contemporary Fiction* 18, no. 3 (fall 1988): 232.

3. Moore, "Maestro of the Language," 5.

4. The "mene mene" etc. are the words that, according to the biblical book of Daniel, are on the palace wall of King Belshazzar during a festival, then interpreted by Daniel to foretell the death of the king and the demise of his kingdom.

5. A. R. Luria, *The Mind of a Mnemonist,* trans. Lynn Solotaroff (Cambridge: Harvard University Press, 1987), 24.

6. Jack Gilbert, in *Monolithos* (New York: Alfred A. Knopf, 1982), 19.

7. Lucy Wilson, "Alternatives to Transcendence in William Gass's Short Fiction," *Review of Contemporary Fiction* 11, no. 3 (fall 1991): 84.

8. Andrei Codrescu, "Style over Substance," *Chicago Tribune* 14, 27 September 1998, 3.

9. Stevens, "Anecdote of the Jar," in *The Collected Poems of Wallace Stevens* (New York: Vintage, 1982), 76.

10. Moore, "Maestro of the Language," 5.

11. Elizabeth Bishop, "Sandpiper," in *The Complete Poems, 1927–1979* (New York: Farrar Straus Giroux, 1983), 131.

12. Robert Rebein, "Descartes du Jour," *Riverfront Times,* 14–20 October 1998, 38.

NOTES TO PAGES 153–154

13. Gerard Manley Hopkins, "Thou art indeed just, Lord, if I contend," in *The Poems of Gerard Manley Hopkins,* ed. W. H. Gardner and N. H. MacKenzie (London: Oxford University Press, 1967), 106.

14. Barbara Kruger, "Pictures and Words: Interview with Jeanne Siegel," in *Theories and Documents of Contemporary Art,* ed. Kristine Stiles and Peter Selz (Berkeley: University of California Press, 1996), 377.

15. Friedrich Nietzsche, *Thus Spoke Zarathustra,* in *The Portable Nietzsche,* trans. Walter Kaufmann (New York: Viking, 1954), 212.

BIBLIOGRAPHY

Works by William H. Gass

Books of Fiction

Omensetter's Luck. New York: New American Library, 1966. Rpt. London: Collins, 1967. Rpt. New York: Signet Plume, 1972. Rpt. New York: Penguin, 1997.

In the Heart of the Heart of the Country. New York: Harper & Row, 1968. Rpt. London: Jonathan Cape, 1969. Rpt. New York: Pocket Books, 1977. Rpt. Boston: David R. Godine, 1981.

Willie Masters' Lonesome Wife. TriQuarterly Supplement 2. Evanston, Ill.: Northwestern University Press, 1968. Rpt. New York: Alfred A. Knopf, 1971. Rpt. Normal, Ill.: Dalkey Archive Press, 1989.

The First Winter of My Married Life. Northridge, Calif.: Lord John Press, 1979.

Culp. New York: Grenfell, 1985.

The Tunnel. New York: Alfred A. Knopf, 1995. Rpt. New York: HarperCollins, 1996. Rpt. Normal, Ill.: Dalkey Archive Press, 1999.

Cartesian Sonata. New York: Alfred A. Knopf, 1998.

Nonfiction Books

Fiction and the Figures of Life. New York: Alfred A. Knopf, 1970. Rpt. London: Wildwood House, 1972. Rpt. Boston: David R. Godine, 1979.

On Being Blue. Boston: David R. Godine, 1976.

The World within the Word. New York: Alfred A. Knopf, 1978. Rpt. Boston: David R. Godine, 1979.

BIBLIOGRAPHY

Habitations of the Word. New York: Simon & Schuster, 1984. Rpt. Ithaca, N.Y.: Cornell University Press, 1997.

A Temple of Texts: Fifty Literary Pillars. St. Louis: Olin Library, Washington University, 1991.

Finding a Form. New York: Alfred A. Knopf, 1996.

Reading Rilke: Reflections on the Problems of Translation. New York: Alfred A. Knopf, 1999.

Edited Volumes

The Writer and Religion. Edited with Lorin Cuoco. Carbondale and Edwardsville, Ill.: Southern Illinois University Press, 2000.

The Writer in Politics. Edited with Lorin Cuoco. Carbondale and Edwardsville, Ill.: Southern Illinois University Press, 1996.

The Best of Intro. Ed. with Charles Simic. Norfolk, Va.: Associated Writing Programs, 1985.

Selected Recordings

New Letters on the Air, 1990. A discussion focused largely on The Tunnel, and including a reading of the section called "A Fugue."

Bonetti, Kay. "An Interview with William Gass." Columbia, Mo.: American Audio Prose Library, 1981. A discussion of fiction, with emphasis on the questions of process and subject.

Selected Uncollected Essays

"In Defense of the Book." *Harper's* (November 1999): 45–51. A meditation on the pleasures of books and the rewards of reading.

"There Was an Old Woman Who." In *Rewriting History,* ed. Heide Ziegler, 69–99. Stuttgart: M & P Verlag, 1997. An essay that careens from the

BIBLIOGRAPHY

Mother Goose rhyme to the O. J. Simpson trial, questioning the relative permanence of historical accounts in comparison to history itself.

"The Test of Time." *Alaska Quarterly Review* 15, nos. 3 & 4 (spring & summer 1997): 69–87. Thoughts about the relation of works of literature to time.

"Shears of the Censor." *Harper's* (April 1997): 59–65. An argument against censorship, beginning with a reflection on Gass's assignment to censor mail during his navy service.

"How German Are We?" *German Politics and Society* 13, no. 3 (fall 1995): 165–72. A comparison of contemporary attitudes to those of Nazi Germany, with a blunt statement of the "moral" of *The Tunnel.*

"Mississippi." *The Yale Review* 83, no. 1 (January 1995): 1–18. An extended meditation on rivers in general and the Mississippi River in particular: how rivers serve as metaphors of motion and inevitability, and also how they escape our attempts at control.

"On Experimental Writing: Some Clues for the Clueless." *New York Times Book Review* (21 August 1994): 3, 27. Argues that much "experimentation" is really demonstrating; but that worthwhile experimentation in fiction should be a form of exploration.

"Were There Anything in the World Worth Worship." *New Letters* 60, no. 4 (1994): 55–63. Argues that nothing, not even an art work like Rilke's *Duino Elegies,* which Gass loves, deserves worship.

"The Last of the Avant-Garde." In *The Novel in the Americas,* ed. Raymond Leslie Williams, 19–39. Boulder: University Press of Colorado, 1992. Gass claims that we now live in a "pidgin culture," a "malformed matrix and misguiding map" that is the lowest common denominator of the cultures that contributed to it.

"On Thinking Through a Little Problem." *Harper's* (February 1988): 18–22. Gass argues that words are necessary ingredients of thought, for which pictures cannot substitute, and that the necessary words are best acquired through reading great books.

"A Failing Grade for the Present Tense." *New York Times Book Review* (11 October 1987): 1, 32–38. An expanded version of his preface to *The Best of Intro,* this essay argues against writing programs as supporting a limited, and limiting, set of mannerisms in fiction writing.

"Making Ourselves Comfortable." *New York Times Book Review* (3 August 1986): 1, 24–25. A review of Witold Rybczynski's *Home,* in which Gass argues that comfort, the central value of the middle class, cannot be reconciled with the awareness good art seeks (and demands).

"The Face of the City: Reading Consciousness in Its Tics and Wrinkles." *Harper's* (March 1986): 37–46. This essay sees cities as manifesting a consciousness, and consequently illustrates some of the correlations Gass sees between two of his objects of interest, fiction and architecture.

"Monumentality/Mentality." *Oppositions* 25 (fall 1982): 126–44. Ruminations on what monumentality is, and what it is not, in architecture and in literature.

"*Ford Madox Ford* by Carol Ohmann and *Critical Writings of Ford Madox Ford* ed. by Frank MacShane." *South Atlantic Quarterly* 64, no. 3 (summer 1965): 421. In this early review, Gass begins to assert the sardonic quality that will become increasingly prominent in later essays, concluding with the assertion that Ohmann's book will "prove indispensable to those who will wish to write others like it."

Selected Interviews

Brans, Jo. "Games of the Extremes." *Southwest Review* 70, no. 4 (autumn 1985): 438–50. Rpt. in *Listen to the Voices: Conversations with Contemporary Writers,* 193–214. Dallas, Tex.: Southern Methodist University Press, 1988. An unusual interview, featuring a comparison of philosophical aims with fictional aims, and candid discussion of Gass's response to the theft of the manuscript of his first novel.

Castro, Jan Garden. "An Interview with William Gass." *ADE Bulletin* 70 (winter 1981): 30–34. Attends at length to the relation between teaching and writing in Gass's life and work.

BIBLIOGRAPHY

Domke, Lorna H. "An Interview with William Gass." *Missouri Review* 10, no. 3 (1987): 53–67. Extensive discussion of the relation between Gass's life, especially his childhood and early adulthood, and his work.

Hix, H. L. "An Interview with William H. Gass." *The Writer's Chronicle* 33, no. 3 (February 2001): 34–39. The interviewer quotes passages from Gass's own texts back to him for his responses.

Kaposi, Ildikó. "A Talk with William H. Gass." *Hungarian Journal of English and American Studies* 3, no. 1 (1997): 5–18. A probing interview, in which Kaposi inquires into Gass's ideas as well as particular books.

LeClair, Thomas. "Interview with William Gass." *Paris Review* 70 (summer 1977): 61–90. Rpt. in *Anything Can Happen: Interviews with Contemporary American Novelists,* 152–75. Urbana: University of Illinois Press, 1983. The most interesting published interview, in which Gass speaks freely about his motives for writing, personal history, and his ideas about fiction.

LeClair, Thomas, and Larry McCaffery. "A Debate: William Gass and John Gardner." In *Anything Can Happen,* 20–31. A debate that has generated more discussion and critical attention than it merits. Gass's replies to Gardner are no more illuminating than his responses to other writers and texts in his other works.

Spatz, Ronald. "Something in the World Worth Having." *Alaska Quarterly Review* 15, nos. 3 & 4 (spring & summer 1997): 9–14. A brief interview on themes that span Gass's corpus.

Works About Gass

Books

Hix, H. L., ed. *A Casebook on "The Tunnel."* Normal, Ill.: Dalkey Archive Press. www.centerforbookculture.org. A collection of four essays on aspects of The Tunnel, with an overview essay by the editor and a selected bibliography.

Holloway, Watson L. *William Gass.* Boston: Twayne, 1990. Labels Gass a "midfictionist," and argues that he tries to balance "the beautiful illusions of words and the nagging realities of the objective world."

BIBLIOGRAPHY

Kellman, Steven G., and Irving Malin, eds. *Into "The Tunnel": Readings of Gass's Novel.* Newark: University of Delaware Press, 1998. An uneven collection of essays, but valuable as the first book to try to come to terms with Gass's magnum opus.

McCaffery, Larry. *The Metafictional Muse: The Works of Robert Coover, Donald Barthelme, and William H. Gass.* Pittsburgh: University of Pittsburgh Press, 1982. Treats *Fiction and the Figures of Life* as the metafictional creed, and gives a thorough reading of Gass's fiction through *Willie Masters' Lonesome Wife* as prototypical metafiction.

Maniez, Claire. *William H. Gass.* Paris: Belin, 1996. A brief overview, in French, with a short introduction and four chapters: one on the essays collectively, and then individual chapters for *Omensetter's Luck, In the Heart of the Heart of the Country,* and *The Tunnel.*

The Review of Contemporary Fiction 11, no. 3 (fall 1991): 7–158. Arthur M. Saltzman, guest ed. An issue of the journal featuring new work by Gass, an interview with him, a small selection from his correspondence, a bibliography, and a group of essays about him.

Saltzman, Arthur M. *The Fiction of William Gass: The Consolation of Language.* Carbondale: Southern Illinois University Press, 1986. Presents Gass's fictional narrators as creators of "vaults of language" that, instead of sheltering them from an unwelcoming world, suffocate them.

Selected Essays and Reviews

Allen, Carolyn J. "Fiction and Figures of Life in Omensetter's Luck." *Pacific Coast Philology* 9 (April 1974): 5–11. Presents Furber as a mythmaker who creates Omensetter as a myth; states that Omensetter's downfall comes when he himself believes Furber's myth.

Alter, Robert. "The Leveling Wind." *New Republic* 212, no. 13 (27 March 1995): 29–32. Describes *The Tunnel* as a "complete compendium of the vices of postmodern writing."

Bassoff, Bruce. "The Sacrificial World of William Gass: *In the Heart of the Heart of the Country.*" *Critique* 18, no. 1 (summer 1976): 36–58.

BIBLIOGRAPHY

   Presents Gass's stories as "not mimetic but configural": they work primarily as symbolism rather than as representations of "reality."
Birkerts, Sven. "One for the Angry White Male." *Atlantic Monthly* 275, no. 6 (June 1995): 112–20. To express the reviewer's ambivalence, constructs an imaginary courtroom debate over the book's worth, featuring arguments first from the prosecution and then from the defense.
Blau, Marion. "'How I Would Brood upon You': The Lonesome Wife of William Gass." *Great Lakes Review* 2 (summer 1975): 40–50. Though Gass protests that fiction follows only fictional standards, Blau argues that even his "most fictional" work, the metafiction *Willie Masters' Lonesome Wife,* abides by "real world" standards and pursues "real world" aims.
Bruss, Elizabeth W. *Beautiful Theories: The Spectacle of Discourse in Contemporary Criticism,* 135–202. Baltimore: Johns Hopkins University Press, 1982. In a long chapter devoted to Gass, argues that, though Gass's essays and fiction confront similar problems, the essays solve those problems with greater facility.
Eckford-Prossor, Melanie "Shattering Genre/Creating Self: William Gass's *On Being Blue*." *Style* 23, no. 2 (summer 1989): 280–99. States that Gass's blurring of genre boundaries is undercut by his "willful disregard for others," placing demands on the reader without authorial accountability.
Guttenplan, Donald. "The Wor(l)ds of William Gass." *Granta* 1 (1979): 147–60. States that the rhetorical quality of Gass's work produces dazzling sentences, but also masks frequent intellectual dishonesty.
Hix, H. L. "Barthes and Gass." In *Morte d'Author: An Autopsy.* Philadelphia: Temple University Press. 41–60. Contrasts Gass's essay on "The Death of the Author" with the Barthes essay to which it responds.
Howard, Maureen. "In the Heart of the Heart of the Text." *New York Times Book Review,* 9 March 1997, 6. A short review of *Finding a Form,* explaining why the reviewer admires "Gass's play of mind" but disbelieves him.

BIBLIOGRAPHY

Kelly, Robert. "A Repulsively Lonely Man." *New York Times Book Review,* 26 February 1995, 1, 17–18. An ambivalent review that treats *The Tunnel* as satire, contending that like all satire it risks being believed.

McCaffery, Larry. "The Art of Metafiction: William Gass's *Willie Masters' Lonesome Wife.*" *Critique* 18, no. 1 (summer 1976): 21–35. Discusses how Gass himself has distinguished "metafiction" from the broader category of the "anti-novel," and *Willie Masters' Lonesome Wife* stands as "a remarkably pure and interesting example" of metafiction.

Rebein, Robert. "Descartes du Jour." *Riverfront Times,* 14–20 October 1998, 38. States that most of *Cartesian Sonata* is overwritten; the exception, "Emma Enters a Sentence of Elizabeth Bishop's," is Gass's best fiction since *In the Heart of the Heart of the Country.*

Rodrigues, Eusebio L. "A Nymph at Her Orisons: An Analysis of William Gass's 'Order of Insects.'" *Studies in Short Fiction* 17, no. 3 (summer 1980): 348–51. Claims that the narrator of "Order of Insects" is not a character but a state of consciousness, "a translation into fiction of Plato's observation that perception is a form of pain."

Schneider, Richard J. "The Fortunate Fall in William Gass's *Omensetter's Luck.*" *Critique* 18, no. 1 (summer 1976): 5–20. States that *Omensetter* is built around the biblical myth of humanity's fall, with Omensetter as Adam and his wife Lucy as Eve.

Silverblatt, Michael. "A Small Apartment in Hell." *Los Angeles Times Book Review,* 19 March 1995, 1, 12–13. Praises *The Tunnel* for rendering the human condition in the form of a narrator who is at once monstrous and "like us."

Tanner, Tony. "William Gass's Barns and Bees." In *Scenes of Nature, Signs of Men,* 248–73. Cambridge: Cambridge University Press, 1987. Rpt. in part as "On Reading 'Sunday Drive.'" In *Facing Texts: Encounters between Contemporary Writers and Critics,* ed. Heide Ziegler, 205–14. Durham, N.C.: Duke University Press, 1988. Shows how Gass's philosophical skepticism informs his fictional use of metaphors.

BIBLIOGRAPHY

Waxman, Robert E. "Things in the Saddle: William Gass's 'Icicles' and 'Order of Insects.'" *Research Studies* 46, no. 4 (December 1978): 214–22. States that, in contrast to Gass's metafiction, these two stories are didactic critiques of habit and custom, investigating "that moment when the average man breaks through to 'inwardness' and then, exhausted, sinks back into banality again."

Wolcott, James. "Gass Attack." *New Criterion* 13, no. 6 (February 1995): 63–67. States that *The Tunnel,* like other metafictional works, is built around an absurd gesture (in this case, Kohler's digging), but its purported focus (the Holocaust) blurs and weakens its real focus (alcoholism).

INDEX

This index does not include references to material in the notes.

Adam and Eve, 22, 28–29, 150
Allen, Carolyn J., 20
Alter, Robert, 77–78, 102
Aristotle, 8, 30, 43, 54, 122, 126–28
"Artist and Society, The," 61, 145
Augustine, Saint, 130–32, 145
autobiography, 31, 101–3, 129–33
"Autobiography" (essay), 132–33

Barloon, Jim, 81
Barron, Jonathan N., 80–81
Barth, John, 76
Bassoff, Bruce, 41
"Bed and Breakfast," 144–49
Birkerts, Sven, 78
Bishop, Elizabeth, 151
Black, Max, 3
Blake, William, 18, 61
"Book As a Container of Consciousness, The," 58–61
Bowman, James, 137
Browne, Sir Thomas, 61
Browning, Robert, 90, 156
Bruss, Elizabeth W., 51–52, 68, 70
Bunyan, John: *The Pilgrim's Progress,* 80
Busch, Frederick, 50

Calvino, Italo, 63
Camus, Albert, 100
Canetti, Elias, 1, 126
Caramello, Charles, 69

INDEX

"Carrots, Noses, Snow, Rose, Roses," 56–58
Cartesian Sonata (collection), 2, 31, 140–56
"Cartesian Sonata" (short story), 141–44
character, 6–8, 25–26, 30–32, 66
childhood, 1–3
Cioran, E. M., 69–70
Coleridge, Samuel Taylor, 60
"Concept of Character in Fiction, The," 25, 30, 65
Cortázar, Julio, 63
Cullen, E. J., 85–86

Descartes, René, 88–90
Di Blasi, Debra, 81
Dirda, Michael, 94–95
"Doomed in Their Sinking, The," 2, 85
Dornfeld, Margaret, 23
Dostoevsky, Fyodor, 88

Eckford-Prossor, Melanie, 35, 75, 81
Eden, Garden of, 22, 28–29
Eliot, T. S., 44, 67
Elkin, Stanley, 76
Emerson, Ralph Waldo, 45, 126–29
"Emma Enters a Sentence of Elizabeth Bishop's," 149–52
"Even if, by All the Oxen in the World," 83

fascism of the heart, 120, 128
fate, 25–26
Faust, myth of, 80
Fiction and the Figures of Life, 25, 30–31, 51–56, 61, 63, 65, 83, 127, 135–36, 145
Finding a Form (collection), 58–61, 70–71, 132–33
"Finding a Form" (essay), 70–71

INDEX

"Food and Beast Language," 86
Freud, Sigmund, 33
Frye, Northrop, 25–26

Gaddis, William, 76
Gass, William H. *See* individual works
Gilbert, Jack, 142
Goethe, Johann Wolfgang von, 69
Graham, Philip, 99

Habitations of the Word, 1, 19–20
Hardy, Thomas, 120
Hegel, Georg Wilhelm Friedrich, 79
Hitler, Adolf, 88, 99, 129, 134
Holloway, Watson L., 23–24, 66–67
Holocaust, 39, 82, 123–24
Homer, 52
Hopkins, Gerard Manly, 153
Horace, 83
Hume, David, 122

"Icicles," 32, 41–44, 49, 124
"Imaginary Borges and His Books," 127
"In the Cage," 135–36
In the Heart of the Heart of the Country (collection), 2, 4, 15, 30–50, 67, 94, 105, 124, 136, 140–41
"In the Heart of the Heart of the Country" (short story), 47–50, 136

Job, 113, 120–21

Kafka, Franz, 45
Kant, Immanuel, 53–54, 61, 70
Kellerman, Bernhard, 88

INDEX

Kellman, Steven G., 79
Kelly, Robert, 102, 118
Kierkegaard, Søren, 100

Leonard, John, 86
Leopardi, Giacomo, 132
"Letter to the Editor, A," 18
Lewis, C. S., 60–61
Lewis, Sinclair, 137
Lincoln, Abraham, 127
Locke, John, 66
Luria, A. R., 142
Lyotard, Jean-François, 87

Malin, Irving, 79
Mallarmé, Stéphane, 69
Mann, Paul, 87
Mann, Thomas, 80
Marcuse, Herbert, 88
"Master of Secret Revenges, The," 2, 153–56
McCaffery, Larry, 9, 56, 66–67
McCourt, James, 24–25, 79
"Medium of Fiction, The," 30–31
Melville, Herman: *Moby Dick,* 79
metafiction, 7, 37, 69–70
metaphor, 18, 27, 43, 93–96, 100
Milosz, Czeslaw, 1
"Mississippi," 27
monumentality, 83–84
Moore, Steven, 136–37, 140
"Mrs. Mean," 32, 37–41
Murdoch, Iris, 92–93

INDEX

Nabokov, Vladimir, 4
narrators, reliable vs. unreliable, 8
New Criticism, 3
Nietzsche, Friedrich, 43, 81, 154

Omensetter's Luck, 2, 4, 6–29, 31, 48, 116, 144
On Being Blue, 62–75
"On Talking to Oneself," 19–20
ontology, 56–58
"Order of Insects," 32, 44–47, 141
Orpheus and Eurydice, myth of, 95–96

"Pedersen Kid, The," 2, 15, 32–37, 41, 94, 105, 141
"Philosophy and the Form of Fiction," 52–56, 63
Plato, 45, 52, 71, 96–97, 154
plot, 30–32
Poe, Edgar Allan, 90–91
Pound, Ezra, 51

Ransom, John Crowe, 3
Reading Rilke, 4, 44–46
realism, 26–27, 47–48
Richardson, Dorothy, 88
Rilke, Rainer Maria, 44–46, 51, 90, 101, 140
Rodriques, Eusebio L., 45
Rousseau, Jean-Jacques, 18, 132
Rubin, Merle, 121
Ryle, Gilbert, 93

Sábato, Ernesto, 88
Saltzman, Arthur M., 10, 116
Seidel, Frederick, 85

INDEX

sentences, 55, 60
Shakespeare, William: *Coriolanus,* 118; *Hamlet,* 19–22, 24–25; *Richard III,* 117
Silverblatt, Michael, 77
Sisyphus, 100
Socrates, 96–97, 139, 149
Sophocles, 52; *Oedipus Rex,* 8, 26
"Soul Inside the Sentence, The," 1
Stein, Gertrude, 63
Sternberg, Meir, 139
Sterne, Laurence, 63
Stevens, Wallace, 117, 135
Stewart, Susan, 79–80
stream of consciousness, 18, 66
Swift, Jonathan, 102

Tanner, Tony, 32–33
Temple of Texts, A, 1
"Test of Time, The," 81–82
"There was an Old Woman Who," 128
tragedy, 25–26
tropological form, 95
The Tunnel, 2, 4, 15, 24–25, 31, 39–40, 72, 74, 76–139, 140, 153

Valéry, Paul, 90

Weil, Simone, 99
Welty, Eudora, 138
Willie Masters' Lonesome Wife, 31, 62–75, 140, 151
windows, 48–49, 93–94, 124–26
Wittgenstein, Ludwig, 4, 32, 98
Wolcott, James, 134

INDEX

Woolf, Virginia, 88
World within the Word, The, 56–58, 85, 86

Yeats, William Butler, 47, 50, 61, 141

Ziegler, Heide, 80